Ron's Hollow

Operating Manual for the Wet Woods

Mark Huck

Contents

Go placidly amid the noise and the
haste, and remember what peace there
may be in silence.

-Desiderata

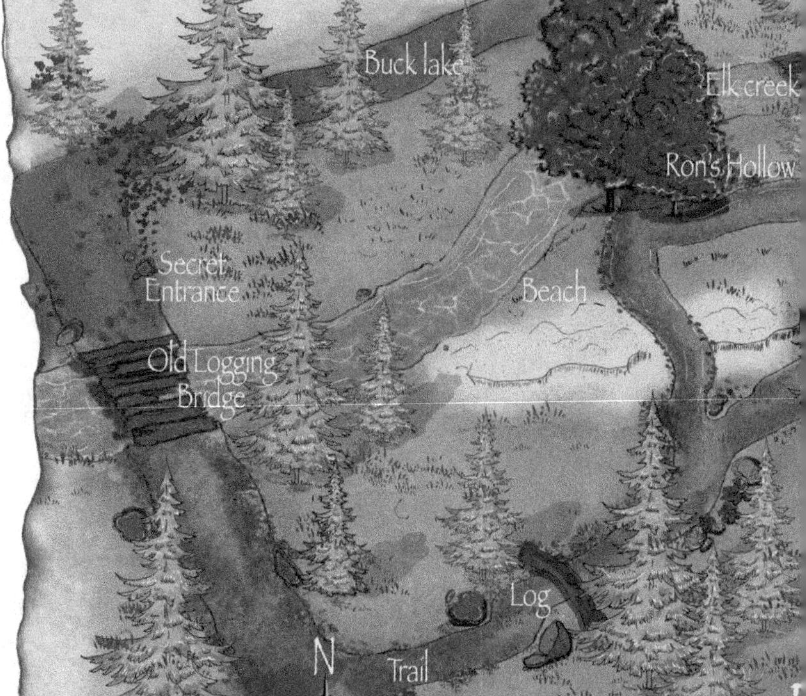

Buck lake
Elk creek
Ron's Hollow
Secret Entrance
Beach
Old Logging Bridge
Log
N
Trail

Nadine Falls
Cornnubbin Confluence
Isabella's Knoll
Huck-A-Lui-Trail
Lots of trees
Land of MARK BELIEVE

North Bank detail

Preface

This Operating Manual for the Wet Woods is strongly inspired by "Roxaboxen", a short children's book by Alice McLerran that I read to my two boys innumerable times in their childhood, continue to read to my grandchild, and which left an indelible imprint. It inspires with each reading.

The story tells of a group of children that conjures up, out of the pebbles of a sandy locale just outside a small town, a subtly thriving hilltop where sea glass is the medium of exchange:

> *There across the road, it looked like any rocky hill –*
> *nothing but sand and rocks, some old wooden boxes,*
> *cactus and greasewood and thorny ocotillo – but it was*
> *a special place.*

It is the story of a magical place, a real place, where wonder is ever present but difficult to see if one looks too hard.

So is Ron's Hollow. This is an invitation to wander there.

Prologue

Ron's gone.

But alive. Ron and Isabella were neighbors on Stumptown Lane in our village. Ron and I spent time biking around the area, wandering onto all sorts of forbidden logging roads. Occasionally we hiked instead. One day, Ron led me on a trek to find an old cabin that appeared on an old map. We followed faintly visible logging roads back along Elk Creek. Then, as Ron peered at his GPS, he declared, "That way" and pointed into a thicket. I took another lick from the flask, offered some to Ron, and followed. Down into the thicket we went.

As we crept closer to Elk Creek, we saw a stand of old growth cedars. Or, rather, not old but *quick* growth. Likely they'd been slightly scrawny when the last clear-cut went along the creek. But, with their ideal position close to a creek and protected from the winds, here they grew large and commanding. Seeing them was walking into a cathedral. You stop, you wonder.

We crossed the creek, and heard a faint buzz of distant chain-saws. This was heartening: in my mind we were no longer lost (Ron had absolute faith in his GPS). We aimed toward the noise not really knowing how we might extricate ourselves if the thicket worsened. We struggled. The flask came out again. Then again. After a half hour, we heard a dog bark. We were close to whomever was working out there. We soon fell out onto the fresh dirt of a new bike trail.

A dog bounded up to us – stick in mouth – and thereafter two sweat-drenched trailblazers approached. They were as surprised as we were relieved. Seeing that its owners were comfortable with us, the dog quickly found a stick with which to play fetch and followed us as we trudged up along the new path toward the beckoning locale.

When we arrived at the supposed site, there was nothing. We poked around, looking for any trace … any outline … any detritus. Nothing. Ron surmised that, after stuff falling and decaying at 3" per year, the elusive hovel was buried a couple feet below our own.

As we were starting back for the village, there it was: a metal drawer pull from a dresser. Clearly ancient, out of place, and in the middle of nowhere. Success. But what had we achieved? Only a small connection with some long-gone cabin happened upon by a surveyor over a century earlier, and perhaps a connection with one of its occupants.

We returned to report our findings to Isabella, full of the usual embellishment and speculation, but did not receive enthusiastic response we expected given the gravity of our metallic discovery.

Ron and Isabella left for their home in the Midwest in March of 2021. A grandchild was due in August – and arrived mid-July – and that together with their children pulled them back to where they had sallied forth to the West a decade earlier.

The evening they left I was sleeping alone with the dogs in the lower level – this is not unusual – and awoke at midnight. Getting some water in the bathroom, I suddenly felt faint and instantly passed out, my head crashing on the door frame, splitting open my left temple. When I revived, I thought the bed was cold: I'd landed on the tile floor. I got up and returned to the other bunk because one of the dogs, Bell, had taken the entire bed. I didn't notice the wound. After a few minutes, I felt nauseous and decided to go upstairs. Reaching toward the sofa there, I called for Nadine and passed out again. I revived to EMTs at my side and a tearful wife.

Later the next day, after an overnight the hospital, time had suddenly became very precious, the passing of time the enemy. With the pandemic raging outside, rest was needed, but where? How? Rest brought restlessness.

Part 1: Place

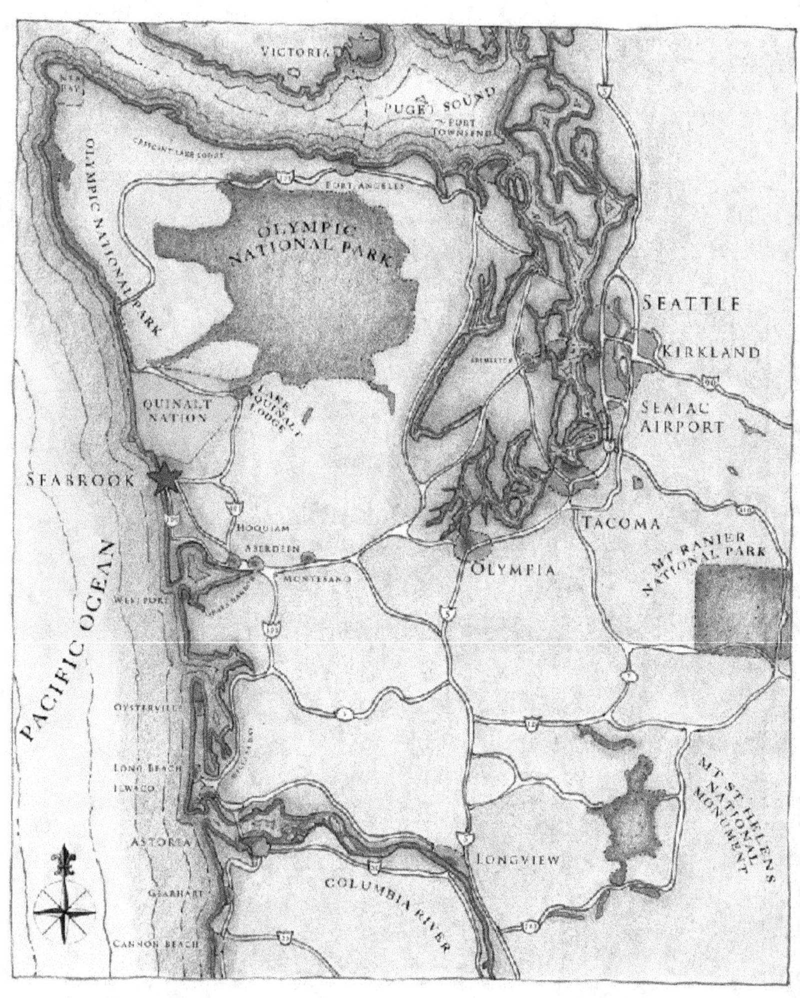

The Pacific Northwest. Drawing courtesy of Seabrook.

The Wet Woods

This is a manual for the Wet Woods, a place of incessant growth and occasional ripping storm. Also, it is a place of calm within majesty, of quiet amid powerful forces.

The Northwest corner of the U.S. is renowned for its rainfall. When it rains, it pours; but, when it's not raining, it's misting or sunny. So, the trees are constantly being fed by water and light, growing to massive girths and towering heights.

Great storms move across the peninsula, dumping record rainfalls without end. The accompanying winds down the great trees and cut the electrical lines. At night, the violence turns visceral, each house in the village clinging to some candles and reaching for calming potions. Dogs tremble under the bed covers, children next to them. For animals and backpackers deep in the woods there is only a hopeless wait.

But, as quickly as they arrive, the storms move on toward the east. Rain may continue, or the sun may warm the day. Either way, life continues its flourish.

Quinault Nation

The rightful owners of this small corner of the world are the Quinault people, descended from tribes moving down the North American coast from Siberia as long as 30,000 years ago. Over 1,500 generations of this tribe made these beaches and mountains their home.

The Quinault were one of several societies on the coasts of the Olympic Peninsula. These tribes included, from north to south, the Makah, Ozette, Quilleute, Hoh, Queets, Quinault, Copalis-Oyhut, Chehalis, Shoalwater Salish, Willapah, and Chinook on the Columbia estuary. All were engaged in an interregional system of trade, marriage, feasting, and raiding and spoke a Chinook lingua franca. These tied them to one another, each having a river to supply salmon and beaches for clams.

In the 18th century, lucrative fur sales to China spurred an increase of trade, but the new traders brought infection. The first incidence of measles occurred in 1779. In the 1850's a series of smallpox and influenza epidemics decimated the coastal population as the virus had done throughout North America the preceding two centuries. Too weak to resist the advance of white settlers and eager to preserve control of the Quinault River, the Quinault – along with the Queets, Quileute, and Hoh – signed the Quinault River Treaty in 1855, establishing the Quinault Indian Reservation.

Fishing at the mouth of the Quinault River in 1913. Photo by Edward S. Curtis

The General Allotment Act (Dawes Act) of 1887 opened the way for private ownership of reservation land, although forestland initially was excluded. The act granted each adult male 80 acres of land for agricultural purposes and 160 acres for grazing. Within forty-five years the Quinault lost control of 32 percent of their land. In 1989, tribal ownership stood at 17 percent. The white settlers played the property game they knew well; the tribes lost.

These injustices still haunt the Wet Woods.

Recent settlement

The major economic lure is wood. The Wet Woods are some of the most prolific generators of forest in the world. With new cities being populated all down the U.S. coast, this timber had immense profit tied into it. The vast forests were brought low where convenient. Fortunately, the Olympic National Park was established in 1938, though this left much of the peninsula open to logging. Logging operations opened throughout the peninsula. One near the Hollow, in Aloha, was founded in 1905.

Logging crew of Aloha Mill & Lumber Company loading logs onto railroad cars, ca 1921. Photo by Clark Kinsey - Kinsey Brothers https://commons.wikimedia.org/w/index.php?curid=67281625

The Aloha mill closed in 1940 as the timber in the area was exhausted and global competition led to falling prices.

One of the central problems of "harvesting" forests is that this is not an annual crop. After a clear-cut, about 40 years will pass before the next harvest is possible. Any economic gain will have been long spent by then. The value of the land drops more than ten-fold after the land is denuded. Thus, this crop is not a sustainable basis for a small town, small company, or lone family. The wreckage is everywhere: rusted mills, crumbling homes, anger at opportunities long gone.

It is a land of shattered dreams, but also of nascent hopes. The beauty of the ocean, mountains, and surviving forests are a strong and enduring asset that is attracting city-dwellers from Seattle to its stark and rugged beauty. One of these new ventures is a small but booming settlement called Seabrook. Importantly for this Manual, the town abuts Department of Natural Resources land on its east side. Connecting the town and public land are not only paths but also a stream known as Elk Creek.

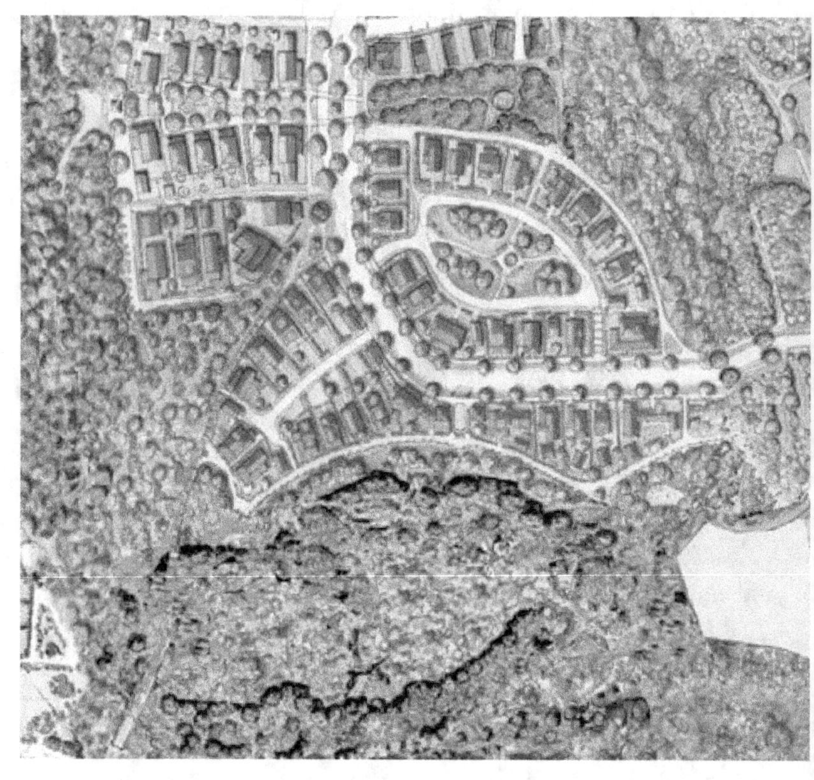

Detail of the Mill District at Seabrook. The fire pit is just above center. Elk Creek is at the bottom. Drawing courtesy of Seabrook.

The Village

The village of Seabrook is tucked at the southwestern corner of the great rainforest encompassing the Olympic National Park. The village is also gateway to the trails leading into the Wet Woods and toward the Hollow. The village was hacked out of the forest by its visionary leader starting in 2004. After 17 years, it has about 500 homes. Many more are on the way.

The town became very popular in 2020 when a novel coronavirus infected the human world. Millions died worldwide that year and the next. People fled from the population centers. In line with state and county ordinances, Seabrook at first turned back those seeking its safety. Then, as the county started to reopen, it welcomed the visitors, many staying for several weeks, even months. Yet, even here, the virus found entry as workers brought it in from other communities. Eventually, though, the virus exhausted its playground.

The village became very busy. It now hums with activity. Free-range children run rampant as dogs bark at them and one another. Construction is in full swing, so trucks rumble down the narrow roads as oblivious bikers zip down the roads. It is controlled chaos; it clamors for escape, for a return to quiet.

Discovery of the Hollow

As the pandemic of 2020-21 raged, I recorded the many official and social missteps that had guaranteed disaster. That journal was unsettling; re-reading it hurt to the core. While I ended the journal in May of 2021, the events it recounted were still being played out. The selfish – refusing masks and immunizations – were recalcitrant, and the death toll showed it, though was apparently of no concern to those self-centered individuals. The old were dying; children were dying. It did not matter.

I resolved, *needed*, to locate a place where I might absorb all that had happened and still continued – pandemic, illness, shootings, inequalities, inequities, and political violence – and somehow still find peace or, that failing, at least quiet. Was either possible in this day, even in a small sliver of the remote Northwest, far from the epicenters? Existential nausea crept in.

The search for the Hollow was also in part due to its necessity. Travel was still largely restricted at the time. As with all travelers, plans had been canceled as the coronavirus spread throughout the world. We were homebound. For some, the lucky, there were places like the Hollow to act as substitute, perhaps a superior one.

The search itself provided relief. Being in motion defeated the cabin fever of lock-downs. Hope welled up. Surely, in this small town plunked in the midst of forests and streams, such a retreat could be found.

Yet, this would not be simply a monastery. It needed to also be a place to bring a friend for conversation, or a bunch of children for some Capture the Flag or Find the Slug. Like Roxaboxen, it needed to be a place of both quiet and activity as the need arose.

> *We need the tonic of wildness...At the same time that we are earnest to explore and learn all things, we require that all things be mysterious and unexplorable, that land and sea be indefinitely wild, unsurveyed and unfathomed by us because unfathomable. We can never have enough of nature. -Thoreau*

My requirements for the Hollow were simple: the place must be quiet, off the beaten path, and by a towering tree. Off I went along a series of bike paths on some extensive public land behind the Village, always gazing toward the tops of the trees for the largest. One path took me by the old logging bridge and near it a stand of large trees. Ron and I had stumbled on this old bridge long ago, and determined that it was useless, leading to where we couldn't hike or bicycle.

The crumbling wood bridge crossed Elk Creek, at that point no more than a foot deep and ten feet across, its water very slowly wending down toward the Pacific Ocean, two or three miles distant. The thick beams used for the bridge's construction were enormous but rotting, missing in places. Through gaps the creek shimmered a few feet below, slowly moving toward the ocean. A misstep and you'd be wet.

Things were different than when Ron and I were getting acquainted with the bike trails a year earlier. The object now was not to be in motion; rather, the point was to enjoy stillness, to listen to the woods and the trickle of a stream.

Then, while wandering down the bike trail near that old logging bridge, it appeared: the top of a dominating tree on the far side of a closer grove, possibly on the other side of the creek. It was April 8, 2021.

Settlement

The first order of business when discovering a possible Hollow in a Wet Woods is to get to it. This necessitated a path.

Having determined that the Hollow was in fact on the far side of the Creek, I made my way to the underbrush covering the bridge, took out a small set of clippers on hand for the occasion, and clipped the overgrowth, slowly making my way across the bridge.

Rotted wood occasionally gave way, but panic ensured success. Thus I got across the bridge.

On the other side, I clipped small branches and pushed larger, fallen ones to form the sides of the paths – curbs would be to imply a construction finesse far greater than that available. Underfoot, years of rotting and decaying forest detritus lent a soft cushion, but also one that could give way. The construction foreman did not encounter this hazard until building the later trails, though it was in the back of my mind.

The first trail led directly from the old logging road (after crossing the bridge) to the Hollow. This route required the final few yards be down a steep embankment of perhaps 15'.

Standing at the top of the embankment, one looks down on the Hollow. Grandpa Tom's Tree dominates a small mossy clearing which is just large enough for a hammock to be stretched between the Tree and a smaller cousin. To the left when looking down on the Hollow is a small pond created by Elk Creek. Upstream, the Creek bends around the far side of the Tree. To the right when looking down is the brush that is now cleared to get to Nadine Falls.

The size of the Hollow and Environs can only be described as modest but amply sufficient to its purpose. Once there, the visitor has little to do but take a seat and listen to the quiet.

Personal compass

The Hollow and Environs require a certain perception of the Wet Woods. One must not be looking for comfort or manicured grandeur. One must be ready to accept the beauty of small, quiet, and tranquil. If that is not a source of nourishment, then by all means turn back!

While the intended audience is myself, no doubt there will be little visitors in the Hollow as Cornnubbin begins to drag her friends there. For these initiates, the Hollow will appear very, very large. Surely there will be games of Hide and Seek as well as Capture the Flag. Yet, I also hope that Cornnubbin and other small wanderers will in time use the Hollow as a refuge for quiet, lulled mainly by its solitude.

So, bring your own compass. You will be guided by it.

Getting there

By design, getting to the Hollow is not easy. Work is involved. Some level of adventure must well-up in the intrepid explorer. Starting toward the Hollow is therefore intentional. Commitment is required.

No one will accidently chance on the Hollow: it is well hidden. The likelihood of accidently meeting up with someone else at the Hollow is vanishingly small. Even if this unlikely event were to occur, there are the several locales within the environs: Hollow, Knoll, Confluence, and Falls. All have privacy without remoteness.

Hiking boots and some libation are recommended. A good book is never a bad idea. If you are also taking a friend, you may want to take a seat cushion as the hammock is designed for one. The Hollow can be cool, though not windy.

There are several connections out of Seabrook to the public biking and hiking trails. As the village continues its growth, some of these connections disappear while others appear. The key it to get to the trails behind – to the east of – Seabrook. Signage displays the convoluted paths of the trails, each interesting in its own right.

If one starts at the Stumptown fire pit, start on the trail directly to the north of the pit. In 50 yards, take the second trail on the right marked "Farm District" and follow until it emerges at the farm. This small trail has its own special nooks, crannies, and spur trails.

Emerging from the trail, look for the barn and head toward it. You'll pass to the left of a pasture. When you reach the paved road, turn right for a block, then take a left toward the east. It ends at a path.

Trail from Stumptown to the Farm.

Go right (going left may be possible if the Narnia Trail re-opens). Take this path south or east, as it permits. Alternately, head straight out east on Compass Street. At the far end of either route you will arrive at the entrance to the biking trails. Continue on these.

The biking trails.

Entrance to Buck Lake #2 trail

The first biking trail proceeds on an old logging road. After a couple hundred yards, a junction appears. Take the gravel road to the left or east and it soon crosses a small creek. You're now about a mile from the Stumptown fire pit where you started.

From here you have several options, all leading to the Hollow. The longest but more interesting is to the left. This is Buck Lake #1. Follow this as it winds through a new forest growing among the decaying stumps of the old clear-cut. The trail ends at another road.

Crossing the road you start onto Buck Lake #2. This trail winds through quiet, shaded older growth woods, and ends at Buck Lake #3. Take this to the end.

Here, the biking trail crosses an old logging road. The junction is just over two miles from Stumptown fire pit [returning via Buck Lake #4 saves a half mile. So, the round-trip is about 3 ½ miles.]

At the junction, take a left and follow the overgrown road down a few yards toward the brush. Look to your feet: if you see a rotted, wooden beam you are at the entrance to the Environs. Here are the two Gateways.

Entrance to Buck Lake #3 trail.

The Gateways to the Hollow

The junction of the bike trails at the old logging road actually presents two choices: access to the Hollow via the Old Bridge or via the North Bank.

The way to the Old Bridge is simply to follow the old logging road a few yards further until you stumble on it. The road is overgrown and so the way will slowly disappear under ferns and blackberry bushes with only the faintest outline of a path remaining.

The alternate is to the left as you go these few yards. To the left you'll see a stand of a half dozen magnificent trees. A log sticks out slightly onto the road to mark the entrance to the North Bank. The only difficulty with this route is that the New Bridge is structurally unsound not unlike its builder. One must be nimble to cross Elk Creek here, thought the presence of the Swing – accessible from both banks – will help to steady your crossing.

The original and preferred gateway for now, then, is the Old Bridge.

The Old Bridge

Hundreds- and thousand-year-old hemlocks and other fir were felled by Elk Creek a century ago, loaded onto waiting trucks that rumbled across the Old Bridge. Near the Pacific, those logs were loaded onto trains destined for mills in Aberdeen and Hoquiam, and from there the new lumber loaded onto sailing ships headed out onto the ocean and toward San Francisco and ports throughout the world.

The noise must have been deafening as the work progressed. Elk Creek would have been an inconvenience, forcing trucks from the east to funnel across the chokepoint. Eventually the hillsides were stripped, clear-cuts ensuring all economic profit was squeezed from them. The rotting Old Bridge and innumerable stumps slowly decomposing into the earth are the memorials to this exfoliation. But life continues. The seeds have already sprouted into a hundred trees where previously one large tree stood. Those felled trees have children growing, some sprouting on the decayed Old Bridge and slowly returning it to nothing as with all life.

So, here lies this rotted Old Bridge, which has now become the main entrance to the Hollow. I'd wager the Old Bridge's builders did not anticipate its current use.

Detail of the Old Bridge, spike in the lower right corner.

The North Bank Gateway

An alternate approach to the Hollow is from the north prior to crossing the Bridge. A branch sticks out slightly onto the Old Logging Road. The path is there. Follow the path as it dips down to the North Bank of Elk Creek. The way is no further than 20 yards, and lands you at the base of the Poplar tree that hangs over Elk Creek and hovers above the Hollow.

To cross the Creek at the North Bank, hope that the swing has been both completed and not stolen. Sit in the swing and it will take you to the landing pad at the Hollow, having cleared the Creek which is perhaps 10 feet wide at this point.

One of the purposes of this alternate route to the Hollow is to avoid an unpleasant confrontation with any property owner to the south of the public land. The Old Bridge is technically on that private land, so this alternate approach may obtain a more secure future for the Hollow. Time will tell.

North
Bank

This route was also devised to allow for a better way to attach a swing to a tree that hangs over the Creek. The path is easy to traverse, except for 3 logs that require a derriere pivot: sit on the log if needed, and then swing your legs over the obstacle. That wasn't so bad, was it?

The Swing and New Bridge

The Swing is the most marvelous and practical addition to the Hollow. It hangs over the Creek and under Grandpa Tom's Tree, serving two purposes: as reading room and as napping central.

To provide access to the Swing, a log spanning the Stream sits nearly underneath the Swing. This is now the New Bridge, and admits of improvement which likely will not happen, the whole being workable if not perfect.

The Swing is best reached from the Hollow. The tree from which it hangs, however, is on the North Bank. Conceivably, the Swing may be occupied via that route, but it appears to be considerably trickier. The recommendation is an approach from the Hollow where a convenient launch pad makes the transfer to the Swing less problematic.

Swing with first attempt at bridge from the North Bank below.

Elk Creek meets the Pacific.

The Creek

Elk Creek is as central as any feature in the Hollow. It comes from perhaps a mile further east, channeling the torrents of Olympic Peninsula rain toward the Pacific. It simply defines the path of least resistance for all that inundates its basin.

But the Creek also tells a story. Near it and other wet, low-lying areas the greatest of the great trees had thrust toward the sky, reaching beyond the sight of those below. But that timber was tempting for lumber mills which needed boards to sell to build human cities on the Pacific coast and far inland, and also across the ocean.

So, while the trees disappeared and a rebirth is underway, the Creek did not get harvested. It has always remained. The berries by its shores provide food for deer and bears. Its path defines the safest locations for seeds of giant trees to germinate, for those trees will have water and protection from the storms.

Further to the west, the Creek finally empties into the Pacific. The Creek's ever-changing delta is defined by the storms that come and go there. No salmon swim up it to spawn: it is a very modest stream.

Elk Creek reaches the Pacific at the town of Seabrook.

At the Pacific, the Creek has become so prominent that Seabrook named one of its neighborhoods after it: its influence is greater than one would imagine from viewing it in the Hollow. Here, the Creek draws visitors, human and otherwise. It invites plans for interpretive trails and creek-side homes. Only ensconced in a nearby sand dune might one happen upon a Hollow of sorts.

Elk Creek trail at Seabrook.

The Hollow

One may enter the Hollow from four approaches: down the trail down the embankment, along the trail from Nadine Falls, via an easier trail off Huck-a-Lui Trail, or from the New Bridge connecting to the North Bank. The embankment section is steep but short. There have been no face-plants yet. Standing at the top of the embankment, the Hollow spreads out below: the Tree straight ahead, the river to the left, and the hammock spanning between the Tree and a younger tree.

This is the destination.

Of the three principle features -- Grandpa Tom's Tree, the Throne, and the Creek – the Tree dominates the Hollow. It looms so large that occasionally it is forgotten in the more pressing matters at ground level.

The Throne, the Swing, and two other hammocks are the only human conveniences in the Hollow and its Environs today. The Swing is hidden on the Creek side of Grandpa Tom's Tree, while the other hammocks are at the Falls and on the Knoll. Therefore, up to four people could take advantage of these modern additions, hidden from one another.

Ron's Hollow, featuring Throne, Tree, Creek, and Quiet.

The Throne

The Throne, resembling a hammock, is attached to Grandpa Tom Tree. Hopefully, any occupant of the Throne will thereby acquire the gentle spirit and smile of Grandpa Tom.

The Throne currently sports two cushions purloined from the Swing. Creature comforts are rapidly overrunning the Hollow.

The Hollow viewed from the embankment. Grandpa Tom's Tree is prominent. The Throne is seen at the lower left.

The Grotto

The Grotto is visible only from the Throne. The Grotto houses the Treasure. Whether it is precious metals, rare thoughts, or better may not be divulged here. The Treasure will create invading armies of marauding shrunken heads. It may well be that it is hauled off to be paraded through some *Arc de Triomphe* to the west. The hope against hope, however, is that the tangible Treasure remain and, if found, augmented with yet more treasure.

All who visit the Hollow will obtain treasure enough.

The Pond at the Hollow

Elk Creek takes a momentary break from its journey to the Pacific at the Hollow. A small pond sits there, minding its own business.

When I stare into the pond and beyond the reflections, there are only decaying logs and branches that had nowhere else to fall. The Pond may be home to none other than the small family of mosquitos that is having trouble avoiding my palm. Yet, its value to the human visitor is substantial: it is human-sized, still and quiet, and may eventually provide a landing strip for an errant bird. It adds to the contemplative air of the Hollow.

The Pond viewed from the Throne.

Barber Beach has been cleared next to the Pond, but does not at all feel like Malibu. The main use of the beach is to stand and peer into the Pond.

55

Sufficiency

The Hollow, therefore, contains the essential elements for peace and quiet. Nothing more, nothing less. All else is brought into the Hollow by the visitor: thoughts, dreams, fears, planning, hopes.

The Three Trees

Three magnificent, towering hemlocks shade the Environs: Tom, Terry, and Jack. By magnificent, then, I mean enduring, signified by height and war wounds. These Western Hemlock will grow to over 200 feet if left alone.

The species is also the official tree of the State, obtaining that honor as much for their beauty as their bounty. Thus, their stature is also their downfall. They are prized by loggers: most old growth has disappeared into houses and paper. Perhaps, however, the boards from the vanished will provide a safe home to other life for centuries to come.

Like the Pond, the Trees draw us and our thoughts to them. They stand, still and quiet, yet provide protection, a covering from rains and a hiding place from predators. As with the Pond, the Trees are simply there. There is no agency except for the release of small pine cones at regular intervals. There is no threat, no noise. We do not share a food chain, though we attack regardless. They cannot defend, therefore we exploit.

But these Three Trees have avoided the common fate of the surrounding forest. They have grown tall and continue to do so, though Grandpa Jack has had it rough.

Artwork by Bruce L. Cunningham Forester

The Three Trees are named for the wisest. The Tree of the Hollow will be Grandpa Tom. This great man was the erstwhile grandfather of our sons. His gentle spirit guided our young family until his life was cut short by cancer.

Grandpa Tom tree is about 5' in diameter near the base, so about 15' in circumference. It stands somewhere around 180' tall.

Grandpa Tom. Note resemblance to the tree.

Grandpa Tom Tree. The Throne is affixed to it at its base (by strap around a branch).

The middle tree – Terry's Tree – is every bit as grand as Tom's Tree, standing in the no-man's land between the Falls and the Hollow. As with the other trees, words are few but actions great. We must listen hard for advice.

The final tree is on the Knoll and has had a rough life. It leans precariously to the east, having been buffeted by the winds off the Pacific. This speaks of my father, Grandpa Jack, who in his final years fought a double battle against cancer and dementia, but remained as durable as ever until the final end.

Grandpa Jack Tree

Other flora

There is one notable evergreen that seems to pop up everywhere. No other shrub is more symbolic of the Pacific Coast than manzanita (Arctostaphylos). It is one of the most distinctive shrubs of the far West, familiar to all *en route* to the Hollow.

Critters of the Hollow

Deer and black bears have been seen in the area, but infrequently. The main critters appear to be bugs: a couple butterflies and a couple mosquitoes, the latter having met an untimely end.

Three different bird calls can be heard. High above the Throne in Grandpa Tom Tree is a large nest, but no occupants have been reported.

Dogs are welcomed. Cats on leash are welcomed by invitation.

The Falls

Nadine Falls are large only to a creature standing no more than one centimeter high. A slug perhaps. But the sound of the water gently coursing over a fallen tree is the sound of the Hollow. It is the only sound, save for an occasional chirp from a lost bird.

> *What a thing it is to sit absolutely alone, in the forests,*
> *at night, cherished by this wonderful, unintelligible,*
> *perfectly innocent speech, the most comforting speech*
> *in the world, the talk that rain makes by itself all over*
> *the bridges, and the talk of the watercourses*
> *everywhere in the hollows! Nobody started it, nobody is*

Nadine Falls

going to stop it. It will talk as long as it wants, this

rain. As long as it talks I am going to listen."

– Thomas Merton

The ground is a soft moss, and the sky overhead shaded by the arching birch and fir trees. A hammock provides rest for the weary.

Perched above the Falls and giving its occupant an excellent view of Terry and Grandpa Tom Trees, the hammock-at-the-falls is a destination unto itself. It has quickly become coveted.

Huck-a-Lui Trail

Huck-a-Lui Trail is the backbone of the Hollow and its Environs, providing the best route to all points of interest. The Trail officially starts at the far end of the Old Bridge. After a short hike to the south, it bends left and to the east. Its furthest terminus is Cornnubbin Confluence. In between are paths to the Hollow, the Falls, and the Knoll. These all lead north off the Trail toward Elk Creek.

More intrepid explorers will create spurs from this Trail into other parts of the Environs, establishing the area as a thriving metropolis.

Huck-a-Lui Trail

The name Huck-a-Lui was the name of our Hood-to-Coast running team at Seabrook. Kristen is one of the Guides (see Appendix A).

The Knoll

Isabella Knoll has a commanding view of the Falls from the South, and indeed has the best seat in the vicinity. From the Knoll, one may look up Elk Creek toward its source, down upon the Falls, across the Creek to a steep hillside, and up the Confluence.

The Knoll has the majestic Grandpa Jack Tree, leaning precariously over the creek, likely blown in that position by one of the many storms slashing the Northwest each year. But the tree refuses to yield. Directly under the tree is yet another hammock. The Falls are heard faintly, and the wind is a bit louder, but the view up the Creek is excellent.

The Knoll is reached both up an embankment from Nadine Falls and from Huck-a-Lui Trail. As at the Falls, a hammock sits waiting for those exhausted by the quiet. From the hammock, the Three Trees are clearly visible, and so those voices are strong. The hammock here is within earshot of the one at the Falls, and so this is a great place for two people to mingle, quietly or not.

Cornnubbin
Confluence
Isabella Knoll

The Confluence

Cornnubbin Confluence is the eastern-most extent of the Hollow and its environs. Here, Elk Creek picks up some steam by the meeting of two smaller streams. The Confluence is little visited, as the enticements of the Hollow and the Falls quickly enrapt those entering the Environs. But the Confluence may pick up greater interest with its western exposure bringing in light denied elsewhere in the Hollow.

Future visitors may ford either stream at this confluence and thereby open up distant lands and more exotic Hollows. For the time, however, the Environs reaches its eastern limit here.

A circuit

A fine circuit can be made. Head first toward the Hollow, then take the right toward the Falls. Continue past the Falls and up the embankment to the Knoll. From there, continue to Huck-a-Lui Trail, take a left, then a left again and back to the Hollow.

The circuit is the active alternative to the Swing and the Throne. Sometimes, a slow walk in a quiet place provides the same solitude as a nap-inducing swing in a hammock. Both may be mixed and matched as necessary.

Stations of the Hollow

With places and trails named for important people, moving slowly through the Hollow evokes many memories as those names are recalled. In fact, the slower one moves through the Hollow – even stopping occasionally to listen – the more intense the memories.

In fact, it is easier to do a full consideration of all these people when making the slow circuit. None are missed, and there is time for the memories to surface.

Everyone who comes to the Hollow can rename the places and routes as they please, of course. It might be a good idea to take a map of the Hollow and write in these new and personal names to give permanence to them. More trees – fallen or standing – can be named, more trails, more mossy spots. Perhaps a new seat is defined and named. Some people may need dozens of names, some only a few. Some places may be named for pets or events; they need not have person names only.

Place, then, evokes memories of other places and times. Conceivably, one might represent all significant people and times within the confines of the Hollow.

The route taken can be altered, or duplicated, or extended, or reversed as needed. Those changes may bring about more or different memories of the same person or event.

If a tree, its branches may symbolized different times with a person, or aspects of an event. Looking up into the branches gives more time for thought, more consideration of the complexity.

The elements of the Hollow become similar to shrines: objects to enable focus and meditation. By having several and moving between them, the connections between them strengthens and new thoughts may emerge.

Time permitting, slowly moving through the Hollow and swinging on each of the hammocks for a while may allow for even more thoughtfulness.

Journey as destination

The walk to the Hollow takes approximately 50 minutes on the recommended route via the Buck Lake trails #1 - #3. Walking has its distinct advantage: it is quiet, there are few if any distractions, and there is a good amount of time for the brain to wander where it must.

Stumps on Buck Lake #1.

Consider the wasteland of stumps about half-way through the journey. These carcasses have become bed for new seedlings trying to get ahold of the earth. Only a few will succeed. But the pause to think about these sad reminders is calming. It is as if one came to pay respects at the cemetery.

And so the journey can itself rises to become a Hollow in and of itself. There may not even be a need to stop at the Hollow at all, the movement along the path being identical to the gentle swing in the hammock. Quiet abounds.

Thus, the joy of a walk in the woods along a well-tended, familiar path. The mind is freed to roam far and wide, even as the traveler stays on the only way available.

> *To finish the moment, to find the journey's end in every step of the road, to live the greatest number of good hours, is wisdom. –R.W. Emerson*

Ron visits

Ron and Isabella returned in late April, 2021. They were preparing their house in the event it did not sell. I'd been texting Ron about the Hollow, and so his interest was piqued. I suggested a one hour break to visit the Hollow. After all, it was named for him. He readily agreed. I grabbed a couple beers for the trek, and off we went.

Engineers relish problems and possibilities. Ron was no different. We made our way to the Old Bridge and then made a short stop in the Hollow where Ron admired its endurance in a place where extraction and development press hard.

We continued, first to the Confluence where we stood for a moment, then to the Knoll. There it was apparent that this small elevation afforded a wonderful if not distant view up Elk Creek. From there, we clambered down the embankment to the Falls where I had to stop Ron's vocal planning for the Environs so that he would hear the mighty trickle.

And so the Hollow was revealed to its namesake.

Membership

Borders are temptations. Borders with paradise visible are great temptations. Swings into paradise are irresistible. Such a wondrous place will create ... demand. Therefore, some membership system is required to avoid over-running paradise.

Initial membership is reserved for those who have a physical feature on the map named for them, and their chaperones. This group is the "initiates." One may also become a member by adhering to the Sacred Oath and meeting the Minimum Education.

But, now there's the problem of over-population. If each of the initiates invites a few more then quickly the Hollow is overwhelmed. New transportation systems must be introduced. Taxes. Government. It's a mess.

But for the present, we can gloss over this existential threat. However, we do need a common set of rules that will bring harmony to the Hollow, hence the Sacred Oath.

Sacred Oath

The Oath is modeled on the earliest recorded human oaths, having a *quid pro quo* to bind all together:

> *[The initiate holds a copy of the Manual to chest]*

> *By the Pantheon, before whom this relic is holy, I, [name of initiate], will be to the Hollow faithful and true, and love all that it loves, and shun all that it shuns, according to the principle that all life is holy in the Hollow and elsewhere,*

> *and never, by will nor by force, by word nor by work, do ought of what is loathful to the Hollow; on condition that the Hollow will provide me quiet and perhaps peace, when I to the Hollow submitted and chose the Hollow's will.*

For this to be sacred, however, we need demi-gods. Enforcers of justice. Thus, the Pantheon is established.

In the absence of a viable voting system, I'm nominating Mom as Chief of the Pantheon. However, she's not invited to the Hollow as she would invariably weed it into oblivion. But, oh would it be organized. If Mom needs projects to stay alive, she'll live into her hundreds and beyond at the Hollow.

Mom will dispense Justice with Mercy, letting everyone in, seeing only good and possibility and potential workers of the weeds. Sitting under her would be the Wise Men: Grandpa Tom and fast friend Terry. They would provide even more dispensations of mercy, hearing the pleas of the innocent.

Naturally, hordes of the curious, many with shrunken heads and known as Cornnubbins, will enter the Hollow. These will create pressures on the soul of the Hollow. Therefore, the Judicial Branch will require a powerful Executive Branch: the Enforcers. For this task, we have the parents and guardians of the Cornnubbins. The Enforcers will ensure the safety of their charges, all while propagating rumors of sharks swimming in the Creek and wild tigers all about, ready to devour unruly Cornnubbins. These rumors will abound in all myths that arise from the Hollow, and collectively be known as The Lore.

The Pantheon may at times become grumpy due to breeches by the Cornnubbins. This is why the Hollow makes provision for a store of fruits of the vine and other such devices required by the Pantheon for its sanity and continuance.

Early incarnation of the Chief of the Pantheon

At certain times, a member of the Pantheon may become so grumpy that no solace may be found. If this occurs, that member will be required to complete a circuit of Buck Lake until such poor behavior is corrected.

Minimum education

Dummies are as dummies do. We need a minimum level of education called *respect*: Respect for the Hollow and respect for its members. Any person not meeting this minimum education is not allowed in the Hollow. By "respect" is meant the following:

- Original occupants of the Hollow – Trees, Pond, and so forth – have the highest standing and must not be disturbed in any way.
- Leave no trace of your presence when you leave. Better yet, restore and repair as needed.
- If others are present, be quiet unless joining a conversation.

It is also likely that the endurance required to reach the Hollow will exhaust visitors into a quiet submission which is akin to respect.

The future

Plans are afoot for a major cultural institution in the Hollow: a micro library housing perhaps a dozen sagacious works. Candy bars may show up there as well.

This cerebral enterprise, being an institution, will elevate the *cache* of the Hollow, perhaps too far. Icarus may thus feel at home. The building will contain a door for the convenience of removing and replacing books. A pitched roof is planned to shed the several feet of rain that will fall on the library.

The dangers of books are well known, and a police force may be required if the ideas contained in their pages incite riots and other unseemly behavior.

The future is scary indeed.

Part 2: How-to

How to: work

Life toils. The urge to toil in order to rest and toil further is strong in all life. The Hollow is no exception.

May 13, 2021 was trail work. Cornnubbin's first visit to the Hollow was only a couple days away, and there was much to be done.

Why?

A great hope is that the quiet of the Hollow may give rest to and re-invigorate others, particularly my children and their children, my family and their friends.

So I walked out to the Hollow by a new route, and proceeded to clip back growth and to complete the wobbly trails between the entrance and Cornnubbin's Confluence, between the Confluence and the Knoll, between the Knoll and the Falls and, finally, between the Falls and the Hollow.

The work proceeded in the quiet. When I stopped, the forest was still. Nothing much had changed, after all was said and done: Some of the short trails were better marked, some of the fallen branches reorganized or removed.

Maintenance at the Hollow

No maintenance is required, at least not for several years. Even then, it will be the removal of a fallen branch and hardly anything else. Future generations will easily inherit the Hollow and its environs without tax or other financial penalty.

Thus, all of us can add our labors to the public domain, though the Hollow is known to few. But beware: a visit to the Hollow with a siren call of maintenance can resemble the walk of spaghetti. It will be quiet yet active, and nourishing.

There's a certain pride in this work, as uneventful and inconsequential as it is. It is creative: something from nothing.

> *A purely mental life may be destructive if it leads us to substitute thought for life and ideas for actions. The activity proper to man is purely mental because man is not just a disembodied mind. Our destiny is to live out what we think because unless we live what we know, we do not even know it. It is only by making our knowledge part of ourselves, through action, that we enter into the reality that is signified by our concepts.*
>
> *-Thomas Merton*

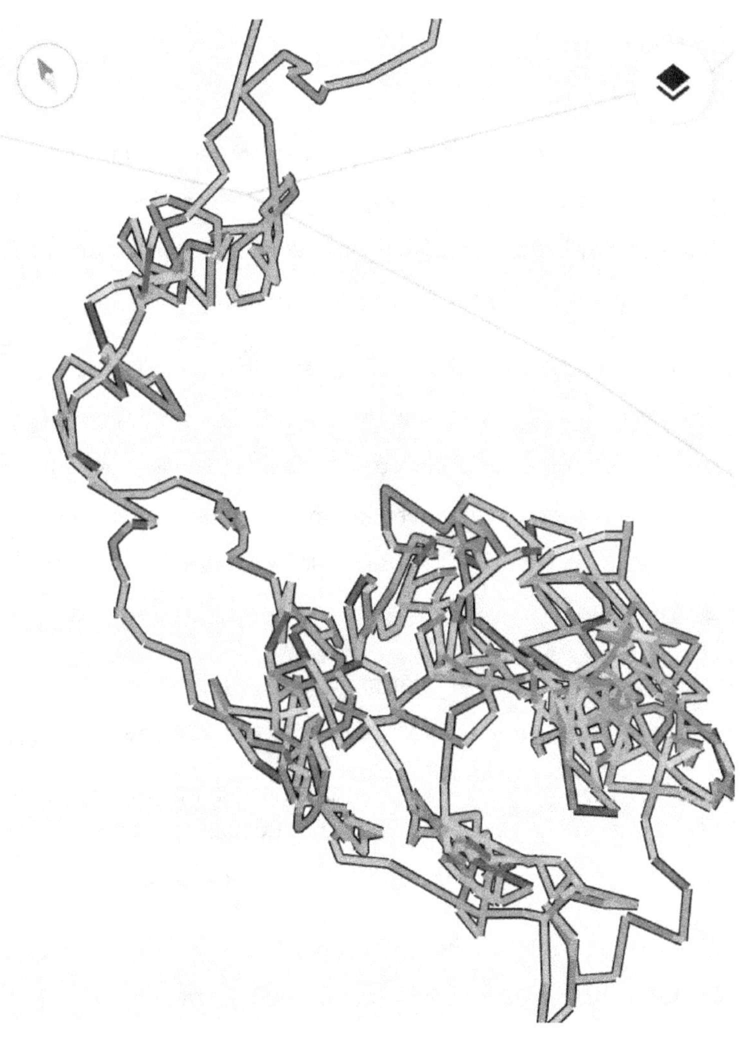

Finding quiet. Garmin Google map of trail maintenance in the Hollow.

How to: move

When we look at a stationary object, we are suddenly looking all around it. When we look at a moving object, we can focus on it. For example, a slowly flickering flame or a sleeping dog's breathing hold our rapt attention. However, a dull rock does not.

Life moves. It moves to survive. It moves to learn more about its surroundings and, by extension, threats to it. Our bodies are largely geared toward movement, both toward food and away from danger. Evolution has decreed that, in the animal kingdom, the movers are the survivors. Slow down just a bit, and the balance of nature tilts away from you.

Our brains are in search of information, of useful information. Movement imparts information. Inert objects not so much. Sitting still, our thoughts quickly go to what needs to be done: in relationships, in work, in survival. Our minds move, even if we are sitting still. It is the condition of life; it is a precious curse.

Robert the Bruce of Scotland famously was driven into a cave on rocks in the Atlantic by the invading English. There, disheartened and watching a spider weave a web only to have the web swept away by fierce winds and the spider returning to weave its web, he realized that persistence was the thing of success. In war, success meant victory. He returned to defeat the English and give rise to the nation of Scotland. Doing.

Contemplation is a luxury not afforded to life. Even the monk in quiet contemplation has a brain busy at work thinking because that's what it does. We must learn to tuck reflection into our steps, or to stand still without agitation. Both are elusive.

How to: change

Change is the stuff of evolution and, ipso facto, life. But change momentarily thrusts us into uncertainty and the unknown. What knowledge we had collected may become largely useless. Therefore, change is not welcomed though inevitable. We yearn for consistency, for stillness, for certainty. When another voyager to the Hollow moved a stick where I did not expect it (it being part of the camouflage), I was suddenly aware that unanticipated change will arrive at the Hollow. It must be embraced; fighting it is futile in the long run. Yet, change is generally sudden or imperceptible. It is rarely managed well, even by the well-organized. For the majority, change rocks us and we struggle to adapt. We tire.

But rest is given to life. And quiet is where rest occurs. The Hollow provides recovery from the incessant change known as life.

How to: see life

They are everywhere: trees and stumps of long-gone trees. They are everywhere in the Wet Woods, everywhere in the Hollow: life and death. And so they become objects of our thoughts.

We live to affirm life, the absence of death. We live to see life in ourselves and in others. That witness to life is the very foundation of any possible happiness, even joy. Life must be an energetic struggle, but one made strong by the appreciation of its brevity for me, its continuity and flourishing in all down through the ages.

To be clear: life requires death. If there was no death, the first life form would have overrun the system in which it existed without any evolutionary improvement. Death allows life to reproduce and evolve. But it is a sad story, always ending in death. The soft under-footing in the Hollow is the fallen life decaying into a rich earth in which seeds will germinate and thrive.

To embrace life, then, is to also welcome a future death. Not to actively seek death, but to appreciate its importance. But, while it is required, death is not welcomed by life because life is wired to survive and reproduce. Death is inescapable, yet life will seek to escape at all times except in final resignation to an unavoidable end.

Death is not sought, except in extreme pain, and yet it inevitably happens. For most human societies, that death must be accepted but not invited. We must be its victim and not its host. While death is dark, it is required for life.

The Hollow is no different: the soft layers underfoot attest to this cycle. Sandstones on the Pacific belie its eternity. While the Hollow is quiet, violent struggle has occurred there, with the scars of the battle evident. Great stumps of old growth trees dot the forest floor. These giant trees represented jobs, thereby food, thereby life for the humans that ran across them. Many were shipped down the coast to help build the great cities in Washington, Oregon, and California.

Most death comes violently. If you are on a food chain, that day may be any day your predator is hungry. Seldom in the animal kingdom does death occur in a slumber. Humans may think they are at the top of a food chain. The recent pandemic should disabuse them of that fallacy. We are a source of life or of replication for all sorts of bacteria and viruses.

Perhaps quiet gives us a hope that life and death will be quiet as well. Perhaps quiet gives joy in this way. But always there is struggle.

Loggers north of Ron's Hollow, 1941, Photo courtesy Museum of the North Beach.

Some who visit the Hollow and its Environs will have overcome the life struggle or been protected from it. Others may be in the midst of a very real struggle, and the quiet of the Hollow provides a small respite. All can have empathy for those for whom such quiet will never arrive.

Life is tenuous. It is fragile, easy to snuff, small compared to the forces of nature. Life exists only because it is able to reproduce before eliminated. It is a never-ending battle to propagate.

Looking at a leaf on a flower, both fluttering in the wind under the sun, life is manifest in all its glory. The leaf is supporting the flower's (apparently) unknown imperative to seed. The leaf fades without water, and springs back with it. Its function is to collect light and photosynthesize. It has (apparently) no knowledge of the process or its purpose. Yet, this is the very essence of life: gather resources so that there is another leaf someday. If that fails, there is no flower and no further flowers from that particular one.

The struggle for the leaf is particularly frightening: it has little control over the resources it requires. Rain may come or go; other plants may shade it from the sun. Yet, without an (apparent) will, it continues as best it know, as only it can do. So, while I watch it, the leaf photosynthesizes. It is amazing.

And so the leaf is one of the most easily observed, elemental forms of life and what life is about. Going a step further, the leaf is not trying to annihilate its neighbors, except as necessary to obtain light. Its economy of effort is admirable.

How to: understand humanity

Over on the other side of the flora/fauna divide and up at the supposed "top" of the animal kingdom sits a person: you and me. Unfortunately, sun and water are insufficient. We must nonetheless gather resources: we must work. But, like the leaf, there are competitors. Others seek to steal my small sliver of sunshine. My work may be overwhelmed by a machine. The struggle is great. The struggle is silent.

Humans are simply another branch of life. To understand human nature is fundamentally to understand the nature of life – tenuous and finite – with a few additional tweaks due to humanity's unique brain and its hazards.

Humans have amassed very recently a capability to hoard or save resources. We can store work in a coin and get food next year. It is a wonderful invention. It is a terrible invention. We now live beyond our use to others. We live beyond our use to life. We take up resources for which life clamors. The young suffer as the old age.

Even worse: we can now live beyond our means. We can use up more than we can afford by our own efforts. We can borrow and thereby burrow into debt. We over-live. It is a natural tendency, but one ultimately destructive for life. A terrible predicament.

In nature, there is no reward for having lived a life, other than to have passed along the gene to which we are largely oblivious. Our old age is the same as a charred forest that refuses to decompose. We are anathema to life. Yet, all life is wired to survive, the purpose being to live to reproduce.

So, every moment of every day, life forms seek to nourish, to reproduce, and to hide. Only when storage is full does eating end; reproduction occurs when possible; unobtrusive activity keeps predators away. As serene and bucolic any scene may be, underneath these three activities are at work. The grazing herd is ever alert. The deep forest is dropping millions of seeds on the ready for a lightning strike. Fireflies flare as much as possible.

When Hobbs declared that life was "solitary, poor, nasty, brutish, and short," he may have applied this to humans only because they are aware of this condition. For most other life forms, there is no reflection on the condition. It is what it is. The present controls.

Herds may roam to new pastures, but that is likely not with knowledge of its whereabouts, simply a sense.

Humans have the unfortunate capability of describing the condition of life, and then more unfortunate fate of having little recourse to change it. Most of humanity works to feed itself in the short-term. We wake up and are reminded of our empty stomach. We eat what is available to us and determine if there is more for later in the day or later in the week. And so begins our busy life of remedying the eventual shortfall. All life is in this cycle, though few species are as likely to complain about it as much as humans. We not only work, we worry.

But large questions loom. Are humans even acceptable to life? Is our species with its vastly complex brain ultimately a blessing or curse to life itself? What do the incessant wars, the global warming, and the anti-vax phenomena say about humans and their willingness to join life rather than rule it to its perdition? Are we over-engineered?

The litmus

The test of humanity is underway, with a global pandemic raging and the response of much of humanity pitiful at best. For want of a simple six-inch square piece of material doubled-over and accompanied by a ten-foot distance from the next person, we have sent a million people to an early, suffering death in our country alone. Other countries have exposed a similar sickening flaw in human nature.

That the battle-line for personal freedom was drawn at wearing a mask is pathetic, and speaks much about human nature.

But it does not tell the whole story because on the other end of the spectrum were and still are an amazing group of people dedicated – at their peril – to healing the sick. This group provides a profound hope for mankind, but the countervailing idiocy is great indeed.

Any group of ten covidiots can overwhelm a rural hospital. And now, to add to the madness, these people have refused the miracle of human ingenuity: the vaccination. What in the name of heaven are they thinking? No, wait, they are not thinking. They have decided that their high intelligence informed by Fox News is sufficient to reject science and, thereby, lead to the deaths of millions of innocents.

We have begun to emerge from this pandemic with the horrifying prospect that humans behave as they have. It is not the first time: the pandemic of 1918-19 was eerily similar. The simple mask became some idiotic symbol of something. It was no such thing: it was an effective contraceptive to a pandemic.

The unforgivable result makes peace difficult to achieve. Time may heal or, as with the Germans, the national humiliation will never die, never be forgotten.

Oh, but there's more. These same covidiots trumpet their gun rights, and so the young die. School children are gunned down in the schools so that the pea-brained covidiots can blow hard and feel masculine. Testosterone is rampant, chest thumping everywhere. Cars get larger and louder, encasing those with small or no thoughts. To what avail? What is this freedom that is supposedly achieved? It is a mirage. There is only freedom in protecting all life by at least some weak attempt at shielding others from a virus I may harbor. Such a small thing, a speck of selflessness, completely lost on millions of completely selfish people in the name of their liberty. Better they seek freedom by thinking clearly for once.

I wonder if the Hollow can soothe such a dark view of humanity. That remains to be seen.

How to: scale

Perhaps the largest failing of humans is to realize that their scale is not the absolute scale of Nature. Whereas the scale of life ranges from thousands of years to thousandths of seconds, we are stuck somewhere in the middle at about a 70-year natural life expectancy. This largely informs our judgment on the worth of life: any creature largely under than span gets scant notice; over that span at least merits discussion. We are a very near-sighted species.

In the cosmic scale, even life pales when considering timelines. The lifetime of a fruit fly and that of an ancient Joshua Tree are, on the cosmic scale, equally infinitesimal. But we are unable to think on that level. We attach too much importance to our species and, more specifically, to ourselves.

Simply moving out a few orders of magnitude, and our life-spans and those of fruit flies are virtually identical. We are but a small type of life that, together with other types, comes and goes quickly: "a poor player that struts and frets his hour upon the stage, and then is heard no more," as Macbeth concludes.

Thus, from a cosmic standpoint, life is important as life, regardless of its scale. This should give us pause. In fact, we are co-equals with all entities that join in Life. The fate of that poor mosquito at Elk Creek is, unfortunately for my salvation, as important as my own. That blood-sucking little fly is as important to Life and I am. Is this humbling? It sure is.

An appreciation of scale, therefore, is critical to appreciation of Life. As humans stomp over their environment, they might do well to consider the larger impacts on the goals of Life versus the alternative.

This appreciation of scale has another benefit. We suddenly realize that we can gain understanding from the smallest visible pieces of life as we can from the grandest. The lichen on the forest trail speak as wondrously as the mighty forests below Mt. Olympus.

It is imperative to remove the blinder of our scale. We are but a speck on a grand timeline. Un-scale your thinking. Consider the smallest: as the Carpenter says, "whatever you did for one of the least of these brothers and sisters of mine, you did for me." Go small!

Of course, this has vast repercussions for the magnifying glass experiments children – or brothers under the influence of older brothers – do with ants. All life is under one magnifying glass or another. If we are oblivious to pain at the small levels where we have absolute control, how can we expect to empathize at larger levels where the object may be in the way to our own aspirations?

Pain is a common denominator to life, from the twitch of the broiling any to the crying baby to witnessing the death of a parent or loved one. Pain stands between life and death.

How to: recover

As life, humans are licking wounds constantly. As we target other life for our needs, we are targeted. As well, life moves on a timeline that ends. There is pain; there is sadness. Grief attends joy.

This pain, this healing of wounds, is common to all. It is inescapable. One would need to live in a lifeless bubble to avoid it. For many, the pain starts early and never abates. These are those we should seek to aid and comfort, whether they are human or other creature.

When the pain is in others, the sadness magnifies. We may be at a loss to help in another's pain. It may be their grief, it may be some loss, and we can often do little other than ask if they need anything. Taking the moment to ask that question is an important moment.

For ourselves, we may be dealing with physical or mental pain, or some overbearing stress, or some great loss. How do we absorb the body blow, get up, shake off the dust, and continue?

First, the dust will be with us. Sadness is added into our life, often a sadness that cannot be ignored or sequestered. It might be the loss of a parent, a child, or a friend. It might be their loss which we cannot help them avoid.

The Hollow is not a solution, but a tool. We may find solace, but we also may not. Some hurt may not be consolable. Such pain may fold into our sadness, and stay there for the remainder of our days.

Our best course is to help others recover – be a constant friend – so that they might have strength to help us when we need it. Maybe, even, visiting your Hollow with your friend can help.

Humans do not have a monopoly on this pain: it is the stuff of life. It is the injury that is not fatal.

How to: rest

When busy, we yearn for rest. When resting but awake, we look to be busy. The act of not acting is unnatural. Therefore, we develop a state of activity described as "busy at rest." We travel, we read novels, we play games, or we converse: we do things that have only a remote relationship to providing for the necessities and, arguably, detract from that provision.

But, because it is in our nature to act, we do things, productive or not. In this doing, we interact in ways that are pleasant and unpleasant. There are smelling a flower and touching a loved one. But there are also traffic jams and demanding bosses, these being more likely in the world of work for the sake of survival. We are more done than doing. In the crush of humanity striving to feed itself, we are very small actors, more likely the bug than the windshield.

There are, of course, romantic visions of work for survival. Gentle hunting and gathering near a gently burning fire. But that is myth. Life is full of predation, particularly among creatures having locomotion. The idyllic work life is simply unattainable for those not born into wealth. Even for the wealthy, though, there are worries about property and property rights. Is someone trespassing on my land?! That dire threat exists, and is the worry of Locke, Hobbes, and their ilk.

Finally, there is the system humans have set up to reasonably provide some food and some shelter to working – and tax-paying – people. That system largely protects us from the worst violence but does not absolve us from the human condition. We must work to survive.

If life works to survive, it also sleeps much of the time to recover and start anew the next hour or day. For humans, rest is one of the more enjoyable activities after sex and eating. If all three of these could be combined it is wondrous. Hence, the secluded beach picnic with a partner.

Wakeful rest is a luxury. Life is not amenable to it. The very nature of continuous evolution and its concomitant competition allows for only productive rest.

How to: quiet

There have been discussed: work, move, change, live, and rest.

Is quiet nothing other than this rest? Sleep while conscious? Pleasant dreams that are reality? It must be so. Rest and quiet go hand-in-hand in the Hollow and its Environs. Thus, the Throne and the Swing.

The human world is beset by voices, many audible. Most of these voices are a nuisance: other people trying to get us to do or buy things we don't care for. These are the sounds of commerce. This is noise.

There is also the noise of social existence: demands from children, calls from friends, emails from bosses, pings on social media. This communication can quickly overwhelm us. When we are unable to meaningfully absorb or respond to it, it is noise and gets lumped on top of the garbage of commerce. As we try to make sense of it, our energy is drained. Noise can exhaust us quickly and easily.

But the greater cacophony comes from within. Here the many voices of our present needs, our past memories – many sad or troubling – and our future plans and worries play a never-ending battle. As this noise seizes our attention, our ability to reflect on more important thoughts diminishes. It is easily possible to enter a black hole of incessant noise and stay there for months and years.

The Hollow is quiet. Yes, there is the trickle known as Nadine Falls, but otherwise sounds are distant birds, rustle of the wind, and that's about it.

Is there peace? No, peace is an imported commodity. It is brought by the visitors. If peace is not imported, there is no peace. But the quiet encourages the peace to arrive if it is carried into the Hollow. Or, if the peace is only small, it can blossom in the Hollow. Quiet is fertile soil for peace. Quiet does not bring peace; peace does not bring quiet. Quiet, in fact, is not a precondition of peace and vice versa.

By peace, I mean the absence of apparent strife whether with one's self or with others. Peace may be found in listening to music, in taking a walk, in petting a dog, in finishing work. It may be found in listening to a child laugh, a friend snore, a waterfall trickle, but the precondition is satisfaction with our own situation. If we want for nothing, then peace may arrive.

However mean your life is, meet it and live it; do not shun it and call it hard names. It is not so bad as you are. It looks poorest when you are richest. The fault-finder will find faults even in paradise. Love your life, poor as it is. You may perhaps have some pleasant, thrilling, glorious hours, even in a poorhouse. The setting sun is reflected from the windows of the almshouse as brightly as from the rich man's abode; the snow melts before its door as early in the spring. I do not see but a quiet mind may live as contentedly there, and have as cheering thoughts, as in a palace.

-Thoreau

The Hollow has two mantras of its own: the gurgling of the Falls and the wind in the Trees. Listening to these can help bring quiet if it is elusive.

Peace, then, does not require quiet. This is a good thing. Most of human existence has sound about it. Babies crying, youngsters playing, rainfall, thunder, music, coffee brewing, friends laughing. Yet, peace may exist in all these and more.

And external quiet does not produce internal quiet. Nor does internal quiet require external quiet, though it is helpful.

Quiet, however, has the advantages of minimizing the distractions to peace. Quiet or approximations to it may provide a safe space for peace to arrive. On the other hand, that same quiet may provide a gateway for internal noise previously submerged under the external noise.

Be wary of quiet, then. It may increase noise no one else hears. So, in quiet, we must be ready to let these internal noises dissipate or, at least, calm. If that does not happen, the external quiet is of no use. Worse, that external quiet may be unwelcomed. It may let in noises we wish not to hear.

This only raises other questions: is that noise that nags important? Is it crucial? Is it somehow related to being *alive*? What is our mind trying to achieve as it sifts through all the stimuli coming in through our senses?

How to: see

Thus, the angle of attack is crucial. How do we perceive things? By what do we measure their importance? How do we react given their importance? How might we act if we attached a different importance? What is the lens we use? What is the measure? Have we considered how we filter our life and the information coming into it?

> *We must learn to reawaken and keep ourselves awake, not by mechanical aids, but by an infinite expectation of the dawn, which does not forsake us even in our soundest sleep. I know of no more encouraging fact than the unquestionable ability of man to elevate his life by a conscious endeavour. It is something to be able to paint a particular picture, or to carve a statue, and so to make a few objects beautiful; but it is far more glorious to carve and paint the very atmosphere and medium through which we look, which morally we can do. To affect the quality of the day, that is the highest of arts.   -Thoreau*

How to: discover joy

Joy is the realization of life's victory over death. It is the appearance of a friend or child after a long absence; it is the beauty of a flower; it is standing in the midst of a crashing ocean; it is the steady snore of a slumbering dog. The feeling that pain and suffering are in strong retreat, that safety surrounds, and that life flourishes all contribute to joy. Each of these may be sufficient for it.

And so peace and joy go hand in hand often, though joy may be found in the midst of noise, as when friends are laughing and smiling, so quiet is not required by any means. In fact, music and laughter may elicit great joy. The heralding of a birth is a central holy day in Western culture.

So, joy must be found in this transient but ultimate victory of life over death. Perhaps in one's Hollow, one must find this joy in the sound of one's own breath. Or, maybe it is the steady trickle of the stream that leads us to consider the wonder of water itself, and the life that it creates and sustains.

If the arrival of life can bring joy, then we must be aware of it. In the Hollow, life is arriving in quantity, though at a speed the animal world is unaccustomed to. Plants germinate and then push through the soil so slowly it appears not to happen at all. And yet, this process is primordial. To give it focus is difficult, but yields a profound joy at the earliest and most silent testament to life.

We don't manufacture joy: it arrives. However, we can create its precondition: appreciation of life, particularly in others, large and small. In fact, the ability to appreciate life in the smallest of observable incarnations may provide the most fertile ground for joy. Spend time seeing the smallest living things sprout. Again, go small! A spark of happiness may kindle the fire of joy.

How to: friend

Love is our true destiny. We do not find the meaning of life by ourselves alone – we find it with another.

Thomas Merton

If friends can bring joy, then they must be encouraged to join with you – on occasion – in your Hollow. Ron's Hollow makes provision for friends with two hammocks within conversational distance, one at the Falls and one at the Knoll. The distance between them is sufficient to feel private, but words may be shared if needed.

Friends are normally those who bring a smile to your face simply by thinking of them. They usually accept you as you are, without finding fault.

> *Let me not to the marriage of true minds*
> *Admit impediments. Love is not love*
> *Which alters when it alteration finds,*
> *Or bends with the remover to remove:*
> *O no; it is an ever-fixed mark,*
> *That looks on tempests, and is never shaken;*
> *It is the star to every wandering bark,*
> *Whose worth's unknown, although his height be taken.*

Shakespeare, Sonnet 116

So, friends who enjoy the solitude of two may be the portal to our greatest joy. Their presence may focus us on that possibility without even knowing it.

How to: winter

Winter is always out there. At the latitude of Ron's Hollow, leaves fall as temperatures drop. Life is in retreat, then it hibernates. Movement dwindles as nature's storms threaten. It is a stillness of dark cold, with fears of losing heat in the storm. Our systems go into a funk. Melancholy sets in.

Warm fires and friends are there to kindle the memories of springs past and yet to come, reminding us this is only a season. The memories sustain, and must be strong. In the eyes of our friends we see the same joy.

It is time to bring outdoor Hollows to the indoors, perhaps join them. Perhaps a favorite stone or fallen leaf is transported inside. We gaze on these as the fire's light flicks against them

The fires burn longer, the music soothes.

We all have our personal winters, and these are difficult to bear, especially when coupled with the dark season. If provision has been made – which often it is not – then hunkering down and riding out the cold is possible if not easy. If no provision is made, then we are quickly cast into a panic that is difficult to soothe. Have friends and Hollows near at hand at all times.

Our Country is in its winter. While a segment of the population seems imperious to the economic, medical, and mental anguish of these times, most are barely coping, if at all. The lifeboats have been launched, but they are sadly inadequate. The covidiots are sinking the boats as they hit the frigid waters. All hands are lost.

Myth of the Hollow

Here is a place that is quiet, remote, safe, beautiful, private, and restful. There is minimal if no upkeep; there are no taxes or fees; nothing needs painting or gardening or security. Does it really exist? Only for a moment. It is transient. Perhaps it has 5 or 10 goods years to it, and then some force will overwhelm it. The simplicity of it is just too good.

But that decade may provide just enough breathing room for some young people, even old people, to enjoy and rejuvenate. It is ambitious. But, there is really no profit from the Hollow. Likely, the wetlands regulations will keep Grandpa Tom's Tree safe into the deserts of vast futurity.

So, the Hollow's reality is ephemeral. But relish it; we can live in this denial for many years.

Resilient Hollows

Hollows are all around, such as one that metamorphoses shortly after 4am when the dogs demand their morning meal. The fire is lit, a dog or two lay in front of the warm flames and start rhythmic but gentle snoring. Some birds chirp outside in a regularly irregular cadence. I sit on the couch with a large mug of coffee. My brain heads off on its unbridled flight through all sorts of times, past, present, and future. The quiet allows the thoughts to organize and dissipate, and new ones to emerge. There is no competition or interruption.

It is a rare time. The world still sleeps. Activity is virtually non-existent. I sit for an hour. Then another maybe.

This is a Hollow that takes little effort to reach. It is a morning Hollow that can only really exist before world starts its march through the day. It ends with the dogs awaking a second time and demanding a walk on the beach which, itself, is a Hollow of a different cloth.

The protected Hollows may be more practical in rains and winters. However, as long as one is warm the need for indoors fades.

A Hollow of a different cloth.

Other simple Hollows may be readily available: long bath, a quiet conversation with a good friend, reminiscing about good times and good people. Perhaps putting on headphones is required, with some familiar music that does not pull us into it, but allows our minds to wander where they must, and then to settle.

Temples and cathedrals can provide Hollows though likely not when the flocks flock. Like the Tree, take in the magnificence and then close your eyes and let your mind move past the day's and yesterday's tribulations and tomorrow's fears.

The quiet of a home at the end of the day is yet another Hollow. After the world has headed off to bed, and the only sound is a dog's snore. Quiet and perhaps peace is all around.

A slow walk on a quiet path is a Hollow, and it moves with you. The motion of walking is so automatic that we hardly notice it, until we get a bit older. In fact, these dynamic Hollows have health benefits, and give credence to "the journey is the destination."

The availability of these Hollows is important. That they are present as required is helpful. Searching out those durable Hollows is effort with a high reward.

Hollows may be shared, even in the same moment. But the presence of the other draws attention and concern, and so may be a distraction to freeing the mind to go its own way.

These Hollows become etched in our core. We remember them, we treasure them. They have given us some rest that is so elusive in the world of life.

We remember these Hollows fondly. Ron's Hollow will be remembered thus.

The Lore

As others reach Ron's Hollow, they may add to The Lore. These mingled thoughts will surely unearth many, many truths from the soft underfoot of Ron's Hollow.

> *Anyone visiting Ron's Hollow may send a selfie at the Hollow together with said Lore to mark@depth.network and the author will thoughtfully absorb the wisdom and consider it for inclusion here.*

From "Roxaboxen' by Alice McLerran

Conclusion

Sometimes in the winter, when everybody was at school and the

weather was bad,

no one went to Roxaboxen at all, not for weeks and weeks.

But it didn't matter;

Roxaboxen we always waiting.

Roxaboxen was always there.

...

And so it went.

The seasons changed, and the years went by.

Roxaboxen was always there.

....

Because none of them ever forgot Roxaboxen.

Not one of them ever forgot.

From "Roxaboxen' by Alice McLerran

Take this guide and go to your Hollow.

Part 3: Appendices

Appendix A: Guides

A great host of characters provide guidance in the Hollow, too many to be described before their appearance. But here are a few souls mingled in the Hollow.

Ron of the Hollow

Ron was one of the heroes of my interminable and unfortunately unedited tome, "Darkest Winter: Journal of a Pandemic." When ventilators were in short supply at the start of the pandemic, he quickly partnered with some former buddies from a company where he'd worked for most of his life on ventilators and with some professors at the University of Washington. Together they toiled day and night to get an inexpensive prototype in front of the FDA. He worked and worked, through most of 2020. We would venture out on bike after his meetings ended, often having to cancel the rides because of issues with the prototype.

Ron thinks, cares, and acts with genius. *Rara avis in terris.*

We had heard of the bridge. We looked for it. Ron was all about discovery and making sense of things. He's an engineer, a deliverer of oxygen. His first question is 'why?' his second 'how do we fix it?'

We returned to the site of the drawer-pull find. We found nothing more, so we continued. We were following an old logging road down toward the creek. When we came to the creek, the bridge was invisible. Overgrown and rotting, it hid. We knew it must be there because the road otherwise ended in a creek. We cleared away some brush and soon the outlines of some hewn logs became apparent. We looked at them, then at each other, and smiled. This was a discovery for the ages. Not sure why, but we both tucked away the knowledge of the bridge.

Gabe of the Grotto

Gabe was a dear friend who suffered and died from lung cancer a decade ago, far too early. A part of her legacy is our place in the village.

One day a long while back, Gabe pulled a kindergarten picture out from her scrapbook while my future wife Nadine looked on. Nadine suddenly exclaimed, "What are you doing with my kindergarten picture?!" To which Gabe responded, "This is my picture!" They had attended school together far in the past. Now, they were friends again. Rather, they never lost the friendship.

So, Gabe had been a fixture in the lives of our family for a long time. She was "Aunt Gabe" to the boys. She was witty and funny, a trait that was strong in that kindergarten class.

Gabe was the hub of a strong group of newcomers to Seattle. She pulled people together, had many great parties, and welcomed all. Nadine referred to her as my backup if anything should happen to her, and so began the tradition of the Sister Wives to be told in a separate work.

Then, in 2012 or thereabouts Gabe was diagnosed with Stage 4 small-cell lung cancer. The diagnosis was bleak. Toward the end, she and her friends all gathered at a wonderful spot, Iron Springs Resort, just a couple miles south of our village. But not all of the party found a place at Iron Springs: Todd and Jess booked a small cabin at a new, growing village just north of the resort. We all had wine and cheese at their cabin one night. The power went out. That was about all I remembered. But, a couple years later, I returned to that village and bought a small house. Today, we call it home.

The cancer took Gabe quickly, but she smiled her wry smile throughout the ordeal. She passed quietly in her home. Her Mom adopted several of her friends as new children.

The treasure is in Gabe's grotto.

Buck of the Lake

The trails around Ron's Hollow are named Buck Lake for a reason. Buck is a young man of ceaseless energy. He blazed the trails; he fought for his country. He owns Bucks NW dedicated to bringing adventure to everyone. Buck is also a mountain biker and competes at a very high level. Just the thought of supporting him in one of his competitions exhausts me. He reconnoitered, mapped, and created the trails.

The Lake part is funny. When laying out bike trails in the Wet Woods, one must be sensitive to drainage. Not a little drainage, but the redirection of cascades off the paths and into some route that preserves the trail. Apparently, after laying out somewhere around ten miles of trails, Buck missed one or two spots. In these depressions water flowed and then overflowed the trail. Ron and I circumnavigated one such Lake.

But, with good nature, Buck decided to call the whole venture "Buck Lake" and went about repairing the flow issues. So, there is no Lake. But the name remains.

Cornnubbin of the Confluence

I have a granddaughter. She's a toddler as I write this. Her uncle, my brother John, coined her "Cornnubbin" long before she saw the light of day, and so she is known. Also: "Nubs," "Go to bed," and "Stop asking so many questions."

She is a human on the move. Inquisitive and active, she approaches the world with gusto. No inert object is safe.

If Ron is the brilliance extant, she is the brilliance emergent. No one knows where she will go nor what she will become. But, what I do know is that she will visit Ron's Hollow with her father and mother, Lachlan and Julia, and so become a part of it.

She has several very important people in her as yet brief life. Other than the dogs and her parents, the next most important is probably Nadine, my better half. However, whether Nanny or the dogs become Cornnubbin's favorite only time will tell.

Nadine of the Falls

Nadine is the mover and shaker. She helped raise my niece and nephew, and then helped me raise my children, Lachlan and Daetan. She is my partner, my closest friend. A hoot to be around, she is so lively she seems life itself.

Does Nadine like the Wet Woods? No. Would she like to find herself in the Hollow alone? No. How about with some friends and some wine? You betcha!

John of the Junction

John is my younger brother. I doubt I'm happy anywhere without his presence and humor. He coined "Wet Woods" when we were stuck in a cabin at Kalaloch Lodge (two hours north of the village) in a pouring rain. We spent that day refining our Jenga skills. The booze did not help.

He is not just funny, he is gut-splitting hilarious. He is also a very prominent newscaster, so has a myriad of thoughtful opinions on just about everything that transpires.

Mom of the Pantheon

The other woman in my life is my mother, 90 years old and the mainstay of the ship. While she cannot visit the Hollow, her presence is there in my visits.

Mom's mantra is fairness. No one gets an unfair advantage. We all must help those less fortunate, with the exception of siblings. So, Mom will bring justice and equity into any hollow, transforming it into a Hollow.

Lui of the Trails

The Lui clan has been an ever-steady source of joy for the family for many, many years. The beautiful – in every sense – widow and her equally beautiful daughters are the perfect role models for all.

Kristen is Nadine's close friend – close as in twin. In fact, they were born three days apart. When together, they run, or talk, or talk while running which has become running while talking. They understand each other as befits a perfect friendship.

Kristen is tough as nails. Full-time tech worker while raising two daughters amid the chaos of a city and demands of family and friends. She brings fortitude and plenty more laughs to the Hollow.

Barber Beach

Kelly has been a constant friend of the family for time immemorial, so about a decade or so. She married good friend Jeff and the two of them provide many fond memories.

Kelly is a running companion of Nadine as well. Kelly and I did an Ironman in Canada together. She'd kick my butt going up the mountain pass, then I'd scream by with my aero-butt propelling me past her and to the next aid station where I'd fear she'd catch me so scrambled for the drinks and left.

Jeff, Kelly, and I forged a funny bond during the Wildflower Triathlon of years past. I had loaded 8 bikes onto the top and back of our car. Then, with Kelly as wingman, set out for California from Seattle. Along the way, a barrage of text messages hit Kelly's phone. No, not a dozen, not a hundred: a barrage. This was Desert Storm.

This was Jeff. Jeff pursued Kelly with a vengeance. A few years later they got married. Nadine was in the wedding party. It was a beautiful wedding up near Winthrop, Washington. Point was and is, Jeff became a chatty and extraordinarily practical member of those that haunt the Hollow.

Tom and Terry

There are two sages resident in the Hollow: Grandpa Tom and Terry Linkletter. There are not many differences between them.

Grandpa Tom was tall, strong, and handsome. His kind smile meant you were safe, welcome, and loved. He was quiet and hard working. Funny and patient. The grandfather of grandfathers.

Terry might have been Grandpa Tom's brother. Oozing the peace of a quiet nature, Terry brought sense, reason, and agreement to any problem. His place alongside Tom is well deserved, if not inherited.

Appendix B: Selected diary entries

April, 2021

Thursday, April 8, 2021

Return from a couple hour hike with the dogs on the trails, reconnoitering for "Ron's Hollow". Find a good candidate for the Hollow and return to home. The dogs are not pleased with the long hike.

Tuesday, April 20, 2021

I head out on my bike to the trails. It's a sunny, cool day. Following Buck Lake #1 to Buck Lake #2 to Buck Lake #3, I stop at the end of #3 at the gravel road and ditch my bike. Heading down the overgrown road 20 yards I reach the barely visible bridge over Elk Lake. Once across I start clearing the brush on the way to Ron's Hollow. I spend a half hour re-aligning rotting, fallen trees so the path is roughly apparent. The hammock is still in place. I'm relieved bears have no interest in the hammock. I return up Buck Lake #4 and sneak through the construction road and back home.

Saturday, May 15, 2021

The Queen of the Cornnubbins (fondly, "Nubs") is visiting with her retinue. Shortly before noon we head out to the Hollow with the dogs. The Queen rejects the royal litter, and so her father and mother must carry her in their arms. Not very convenient.

We meander the wrong way down Buck Lake #4. The belly-aching starts early: how much further? That sure is a long mile!

I take a mental note to make sure adults have adult beverages before undertaking this journey. The dogs and Queen, on the other hand, are having a grand old time.

Lo and behold, we arrive at the Bridge. I take Stan across first and he is not careful about the large, gaping holes in the bridge and nearly falls in. I pull him back to safety and we all get across.

We head up the trail. I rightly avoid the Hollow Express trail as it has a steep grade down the embankment. We head down Huck-a-Lui toward the Confluence. Already, doubts and griping are coming forth from the cheap seats. The retinue is not letting the Emperor have her new clothes.

After a brief survey of the Confluence, we make the tiny climb up the Knoll. Again, little appreciation for the utter sanctity of the Hollow and its Environs. Getting down the embankment to Nadine Falls does not help matters. In fact there's a general mutiny. After quelling this insurrection, we get everyone to the Falls. All are underwhelmed.

It's a quick trek to the Hollow. In the ultimate insult, Stan decides this is where to do his business. I can see that this tour is not the fine reception received from Ron (see "Revelation" above).

Rather than climb the embankment, the retinue with Queen bush-whack a round-about way to the Huck-a-Lui trail. I make another mental note that this will be the first improvement on my next return.

On the way back I remark that at least they know where to find me should I not return some day. A cheery thought, but practical.

More important: the Queen has visited the Hollow.

Tuesday, May 18, 2021

Driven by the demand to improve the customer experience, I head out to the Hollow. First, I head up Buck #3 a bit to find another possible candidate for a retreat that does not involve a bridge. I see a tree that might act as the lodestone, and veer off the trail and into the thicket. After bush-whacking for about 20 minutes, I hit a thick brush and decide that there is not an easy solution, so return to the trail and head toward the bridge.

First order of business is to create the 3 switchbacks to the Hollow so that the retinue can pass safely. I reorganize fallen saplings so that this trail is visible, then mosey the few steps to Nadine Falls.

It is apparent that this is truly the best locale in the Hollow and its Environs. The gentle trickle of the Falls, the moss underfoot, and the sparkle of sun hitting the creek. It only needs a bed.

How to go recumbent here? I think perhaps a fold-up chair. But maybe a simple towel would suffice to ensure the damp floor would not soak through one's pantaloons.

What's more: it is here that I see where the JM Wine Cellar must go.

A wine rack would fit nicely in this cove at the Falls.

Saturday, May 22, 2021

Today was the first avowed visit to the Hollow without the express purpose of changing or improving anything. I thought perhaps 20 minutes of quiet might be a good start for a hardened Westerner. "Ye shall know them by their works." "Idle hands are the devil's playground." Etc.

The truly desirable spot is at the Falls where the roaring trickle creates a mesmerizing sound complemented by the wind through the trees and a few birds. Those are the three sounds. I found the thick root of a large tree on the steps up to the Knoll, and sat there. It was very comfortable for my needs, and I looked all about wondering at what thoughts would come to mind.

The first was an ever-attentive listening to the sounds, but more so for sounds that might be threats. There were none. So I continued to listen.

My mind would not get off the listening to the 3 sounds: water, wind, and birds while looking all around at the water and trees, I didn't come here with the idea of thinking about something in particular, just wondering where my attention would focus.

Saturday, May 29, 2021

On the way to the Hollow, I spy 2 trees on the far side of the Creek that may provide an alternate refuge: Bulls Hollow. To get there, however, will take a lot of bushwhacking and fjording. This will be for another day.

I continue to the Hollow, plop onto the Throne, pull out my pen and a draft of the Manual, and start writing, accompanied by a lone fly that must think I'm lunch.

I then decide to circumnavigate Grandpa Tom Tree. I start via the east side, and quickly see the Creek on the north side. I move closer to the Creek and there, looming above the Creek and leaning over it from the opposite bank, is a formidable poplar tree, its lower branches reachable to me.

This will be – must be – the apparatus for the Swing which I now endeavor to build at some point. Construction, therefore, has begun in my mind.

I return to the Throne and start to drink a beer that had fallen into my daypack. I then circumnavigate a second time to make further mental notes which I resolve to record lest they dissolve. The launch and landing spot for the Swing is perfectly situated for construction and use.

This location may also be a good spot for a second access to the Hollow, all then being on public land. The Bridge is on private land even though the Hollow is on public.

Leaving the Hollow, I keep looking back trying to see the top of the Tree. The best view is at the start of the Bridge. From there I'll deploy my first use of high school geometry ever in order to calculate the Tree's height: side-angle-angle or something like that. It's been a half century since that formula was used by me.

June, 2021

Tuesday, June 8, 2021

After receiving a draft copy of "Ron's Hollow", Ron replies in text: "please work in 'ruggedly handsome' and 'chiseled physique.'" I thought this was assumed when I explained that he was an engineer. Anyway, so it is. He goes on to comment:

> In addition to being "present" with the quiet
> sounds, my mind always goes to the history when
> visiting a place.

I always wonder: what has the Hollow seen as a living thing? … It's been home to other life. Has seen glacial runoff. Tidal waves that caused the "ghost forest." Buildup of detritus we thought maybe a ¼ inch per year is 3 feet deep since the bridge was built. I wonder who rode over the bridge and layer it in. What was their story, where did they grow up? Where did they end up?

We as humans are poor time travelers. We are not dogs who can sniff the history of a random piece of wood. We are religiously focused on the present and fearful of tomorrow. The simple ability to pass along history of any sort came with language and, later, writing. But that history might equate to co-existent peace and violence, growth and destruction. Can we hold those at the same time? It is difficult.

Thursday, June 10, 2021

I sit with a neighbor and his children around a campfire and present them advance drafts of "Ron's Hollow." These are the types of energetic youth that my actually attempt to find the place. But that family heads out of town and won't be back until the beginning of July. The Hollow is safe until then.

Saturday, June 12, 2021

Having been snubbed by the Lui teenagers for a visit to the Hollow, I take off on a run there. My purpose, however, is one of engineering: to find an access to the north bank of Elk Creek at the Poplar tree directly across from the Hollow.

Having run along Buck Lake trails 1-3, I arrive at the old logging road, a little over 2 miles from Stumptown. Rather than cross the Bridge, I veer into the stand of large trees to my left and, eyeing Grandpa Tom Tree, head in that direction. A path is easy to make and I'm soon at the base of the Popular tree, having passed by the eerie rotted stump of an tree felled perhaps a hundred years earlier. New trees sprout from the top of its now jagged top.

Access to the Poplar tree from this route will allow for an easy attachment of the swing – ordered a few days ago – to the tree. The rope can then be grabbed from the landing pad on the other side, allowing the user to either simply sit and swing with the Creek below or access the Hollow.

With this engineering feat of monumental proportions – blazing the trail to the North Bank – now completed, the next question is one of next steps. The enterprise will be threatened if the chief engineer ends up in the drink during construction. I resolve to have a good rope for hanging the swing.

On my next visit, I'll bring some hand-clippers to better clear the underbrush. Perhaps I will locate an appropriate spot for the rope.

Monday, June 14, 2021

After a morning meeting, I return to the North Bank to clear the trail. The day is warm, and the effort goes quickly. The visitor will be required to step over three large branches, but those are the only obstacles. I return home to draw a more detailed map of this approach to the Hollow.

Wednesday, June 16, 2021

Swing day! After breakfast, I head to the North Bank with the contraption. While it was billed as an outdoor convenience, it is not made of nylon and so I figure it'll only last a couple seasons. I get to the Poplar tree on the North Bank, stretch up and onto the first branch. From there I wrap a nylon strap around the trunk, then get the swing, attach it, and ... the pillows fall in the Creek. I fish them out with a long branch, then head up and around over the Bridge to the South Bank and make my way to the landing pad by Grandpa Tom Tree. It's easy to grab the swing, but the task of actually getting into it looks daunting since one would the swing across the Creek and into the Poplar tree.

So I fish a sizable log out of the Creek, and test it for strength. Appears solid enough. I wrestle it so it lands across the Creek almost directly under the Swing. Perfect! Well, good enough. I can step out onto the log, grabbing the Poplar branch above and ease into the swing.

The clearance to the Creek when the Swing is fully loaded is about 8 inches or so. I assume this will need to be increased as the fabric stretches.

Looking downstream, sunlight pokes through the canopy and it is a pleasant view. Looking upstream, though, the view is darkened by the canopy, and it is eerie. I resolve to sit facing downstream when I return again.

Looking downstream from the Swing.

Friday, June 18, 2021

Early morning jog to the Hollow with sole purpose to sit and perhaps write. And listen.

The beach is only 10' from the Throne, but no sun on it at 10:10. All available sunlight is harnessed by the green above.

The wind is blowing in the upper branches, but it is still in the Hollow. The wind drown out the Falls.

The sun barely breaks through the branches and needles of Grandpa Tom Tree to reach the Hollow.

Ferns grow at my feet, and there are grasses over by the pond.

I lay down in the hammock Throne for the first time, making use of the pillows from the Swing, and am staring up toward the invisible top of the Tree. I estimate at the base it's 5-6' in diameter.

A foot above my head a small spider is working. I see one shimmering web thread stretching across the Hollow.

A mosquito meets an untimely end.

All the branches are swaying far up. I have a need to notice things.

Sunlight pokes through to the Hollow.

Trigonometry may help me figure out the height of Grandpa Tom's Tree. From the north side of the old logging bridge, I estimate that I'm 40' from the tree and the top appears to be at a 75-degree angle. Therefore, my first guess of its height is 149'.

Monday, June 21, 2021

Morning jog to the Hollow. Took clippers to clear the Beach.

Thought about all the tools humans schlep around. I suppose clothes are a tool, so there's that. Then there's: shoe laces; a phone with camera; a watch with GPS, pulse, and elevation. Oh, and a clock. There's the clippers. No water bottle today, but a bottle is a tool. Finally, a hat with a visor. All stuff a gorilla does not carry about.

Got to the Hollow and cleared the beach. Some good sun hits it at about 11am, but probably will disappear early afternoon.

Does the Beach now qualify the Hollow as a resort? t/b/d.

After the requisite work permitting, according to the Protestant Work Ethic, a reset, I mosey over to the Swing.

I uneasily move along the New Bridge, grasping the Poplar's branch. I rearrange the Swing to look both downstream and a bit toward Grandpa Tom Tree.

This is a good positioning. It being the day after Father's Day, I do a little reminiscing about Tom. He was so quiet, yet always doing something. Bucking hay. Taking my boys fishing, building something. But a quiet man. Tall, lean, and a welcoming twinkle in his eye.

Thought also about my dad, known to some as Jack. Very similar to Tom in many ways. Always there and helping. Never asking for anything. Ready with a joke and a smile.

But construction noise from the far-off Village filters through. I gather my few tools and walk back. Even a short stay is a good one.

Monday, June 28, 2021

Jogged out to the Hollow in the last blistering heat of a record hot spell in the Northwest. The Hollow was cool, but no wind. One mosquito met its maker, but its horsefly compatriot hounded me on most of my return to civilization.

Wednesday, July 14, 2021

Jogged out to the Hollow and, on the way, had an idea for a "Race to Ron's Hollow", the proceeds benefiting Paws of Grays Harbor and the Seattle Animal Shelter. Will propose this to the Seabrook people. All participants may submit their thoughts about the Hollow, and I'll edit these for inclusion in the book. This officially makes Ron's Hollow participatory. I wonder if this is a good thing.

Why a race? First, to perhaps support local animal shelters. Second, though, is to lead people to the Hollow on their own.

Potential prizes? Chocolate, of course. There will be a leaderboard. Where to put it? Ronshollow.com, so I secure the domain.

Will this idea bring ruin to the Hollow? Perhaps, and for this reason I will think more on it.

Wednesday, July 21, 2021

After a run out to the Hollow, I pack the dogs into the car and we head to Ocean Shores to get tools for the Hollow: a garden rake to begin manicuring the trails, and a saw to clear away some larger logs. All in the name of progress. Also under consideration: trail signs. These need to be natural, durable, and cheap: my usual standard for any purchase. I'm thinking of a tool for simply burning the name on a plank of wood. That should do. A quick search and I see "Burnmaster HAWK" – so manly. I also see that there is a technical name for this art: pyrography. Sounds like a possible addition to my resume. I can probably use cedar grilling planks. Apparently, nailing into healthy trees is OK – the tree heals around the wound – but nailing into unhealthy trees is not OK.

I foresee much trail maintenance in my future.

Thursday, July 22, 2021

Deliver saw and rake to the Hollow, the first implements there. As foreseen, do about an hour's worth of trail maintenance leading to a long rest on the Throne. After that, head to Nadine Falls where I determine this might be a great locale for another hammock: the Falls are mesmerizing.

Is this what humans do, incessantly seek out ways to improve? I anticipate that every other trip to the Hollow will have some maintenance involved.

Maintenance spaghetti. This does not look like calm but is quiet.

Later, I order two hammocks, one for the Falls and one for perhaps the Knoll. This will bring the hammock plus swing total to 4. Development is underway; overpopulation a threat.

Signs

Wednesday, July 28, 2021

Biked to the Hollow for the installation of signs and Falls hammock.

Hammock at the Falls

Friday, July 30, 2021

Installed additional signs and discovered the pleasures of multiple circuits from the Hollow to Nadine Falls to the Huck-a-Lui Trail (via the Knoll) and back around to the Hollow. While the circuit is barely a couple hundred yards, the ups and downs make it a hardy hike.

August, 2021

Monday, August 2, 2021

Catherine and John visit for my birthday, and I drag John out to the Hollow on our bikes. He sees my vision for Cornnubbin and her friends, I think. It is a great comfort.

Monday, August 8, 2021

At 4:30am dogs have been fed and I'm in the Hollow of the living room with the dogs, fire softly burning. My thoughts go, as always, to relationships, then work. Who am I forgetting? Who should I be in contact with about something? How can I mend bridges still burning? What urgent matters must be done today, now?

After my usual 9am meeting with Rachel, I head out on a run to the Hollow. It survived the weekend rain; how could it not? What is there to destroy? The hammock pillows are wet, that's all. I do the circuit by the Falls – the waterfall is no larger or smaller, just there – and then up to the Knoll and around to the exit. I stop and one point and walk a few steps away from the Environs. I look around. All is still, and safe from my improvement.

Thursday, August 19, 2021

Two days ago was a red-letter day: the daughter of Nadine's colleague requested a visit to the Hollow. I promptly provided her a draft copy of Ron's Hollow, and we set up a visit for Sunday.

Then, yesterday, we were having some wine with Mike and Heather when the conversation veered to the biking trails and then to Ron's Hollow. Looks like they'll be joining the Sunday tour as well.

Today I ran out to the Hollow and walked the circuit. Apparently, spiders also lurk in the Hollow. There was something very comforting in seeing the Hollow exactly as I had left it a few days earlier, and yet I'd done no cleaning or other upkeep, and had not had to pay any utilities or rent. I did empty pine needles from the hammocks.

Saturday, August 21, 2021

The Barbers are in town. Kelly and I run to the Hollow and inspect Barber Beach. We discuss the ambiguities of "Nadine Falls", recalling the many face-plants of our trail running adventures. I comment that the ambiguity would have to apply to Victoria Falls, for example, though perhaps Queen Victoria had stability issues as well.

Sunday, August 22, 2021

This is the big day, a day like no other. Hordes of 5 people – me included – will venture across the many obstacles and past numerous diversions to get to the Hollow. The promise is huge. The weather looks like it will cooperate.

But ... zounds! ... work interrupts the mother and her child, so only Kelly drags Jeff to the Hollow. No population explosion yet.

Wednesday, August 25, 2021

Spend a whole day in a different Hollow: doing the 19 miles of High Divide over by Sol Duc. It is naturally all work and all forward motion. The day is perfect and the views extraordinary.

Is the high meadow overlooking Mt. Olympus a Hollow? I think so. Certainly, there was quiet and solitude alongside the majestic beauty. Was the entire 8 hour trip a Hollow? Perhaps. However, this Hollow is inconvenient to reach and finish, though the memories from it are strong.

Tuesday, August 31, 2021

Provide a draft of Ron's Hollow to Buck and some Seabrook Powers for comment. Hope the blow back is not too stiff. Later in the afternoon, run to the Hollow and install the 3rd and final hammock up on the Knoll. Need to test its durability under pressure a bit. Its location allows one to see all three trees and hear the Falls. Sweet!

So, now I have this strange feeling of fear about something that was never mine. The Hollow is little more than a state of mind, but I wonder why I feel the way I do. Strange. Perhaps human.

September, 2021

Monday, September 6, 2021

Labor Day.

I stopped a daily journal of the pandemic four months ago. Then, it was clear that, if the vaccines were distributed effectively, the pandemic would end in the U.S. However, the game has played out differently. The 1/3 of the country that refused vaccines is now being inoculated by another route: the Delta variant. But I'm resigned that it is too late to help these people. The virus will blow through their communities before anything can be done. Even now, the new variant is running out of targets. While sad, this brings peace. It is essentially over.

It is also the last crazy summer day in the Village. I may visit the Hollow if a dare run the gauntlet to get there. But the beautiful day is enticing. I imagine relaxing in the Knoll's hammock, listening to the slow trickle of Nadine Falls.

Pratt's Hollow

Our friends, Michael and Heather, invite us to walk on the beach to Copalis Rocks. We leave at 2pm and return at 6pm. It's a wonderful hike at the very edge of the continental U.S. We cross Elk Creek's mouth twice as we make our way. Today, the waters are pleasantly cool after being warmed most of the day in a late summer respite.

Tuesday, September 7, 2021

Jog to the Old Bridge and walk into the Hollow. All is well. It is quiet. The trickle of the Falls can be heard throughout the Environs. I adjust the hammock at the Knoll, and lay down in it. Faintly visible is Grandpa Tom Tree at the western end of the Environs. Looming my face is Grandpa Jack tree, its scarred trunk next to me. The tree leans a good 10 degrees to the north. I wonder how it is still standing. I also wonder what happened to scar its bark at the base. Whatever it was, it wasn't fatal.

From the hammock on the Knoll, I look down at the hammock at the Falls. This would be a great place to relax with a friend, enjoying the quiet and an occasional observation. With this observation, I think I've stumbled on a social dimension to the Hollow: it allows for full attention to whomever you're with.

Tuesday, September 21, 2021

This may be an old age thing. Ran to the Hollow and did the Stations. But, at most, I simply looked at things without any thoughts going through my mind, except the thought that I had no thoughts. It felt good.

So, simply visiting the Hollow brings satisfaction. Gazing on familiar and pleasant things, even without reflecting on them, is valuable in itself. I need not bring anything to the Hollow; it presents things to me. Simply by *being*, these things bring a sense of happiness. I need not add anything; they need not say anything. In those moments of transaction-free existence, the feeling is one of inhaling and exhaling deeply after a busy day.

Thursday, September 23, 2021

The fogs burn off in the early afternoon and I walk to the Hollow. It's cooler, so I'm dressed in a sweatshirt and long pants. Getting there is about 50 minutes, but is very rewarding. The journey feels like a Hollow. There is little to distract my mind but to follow the winding paths toward that spot.

Once there, I immediately head to the hammock on the Knoll. Having a sweatshirt on, I'm able to cocoon myself in the hammock, and simply rock with whatever motion remains of my flop into the pod. I look up: it is the only direction available. A nap would be good, but it does not come.

Thursday, September 30, 2021

A tempest blew across the coast yesterday and last night, inundating the Wet Woods, but the skies begin to clear in midafternoon. Wanting to test out a pair of trail shoes I'll be taking on the High Divide next week, I set out on a walk to the Hollow. The roar of the ocean follows me into the woods.

Along Buck Lake #1 I am met with the sounds of innumerable streams emptying their contents toward the sea. The trails are in great shape. Buck and the Evergreen Trails people have nailed it.

On Buck Lake #3, I round a corner and a large black bear scurries off down the trail. He or she doesn't even look at me, but disappears into the woods to the right of the trail. A few hundred yards further – before the bridge on the trail – a glance to the left reveals what appears to be a small trail. I can hear a stream – perhaps part of Elk Creek – and it pulls me in.

I follow the primitive trail a few yards and then see that it's indeed an intentional path: the remains of a wood quarry are here. Industry in the Wet Woods! A stack of hewn pieces is near a butchered stump, their use likely as firewood, though some of the pieces seem thin enough to be the first makings of a table.

I pick up a small remnant to take to the Hollow, aiding and abetting the theft.

The wood quarry.

Returning to the main trail, I wonder who was here, deep in the woods, and how the lumberjacks might have removed their wood without the benefit of the trails which were only built a year earlier. Perhaps it was a worker on the trail, and this was part of the end-of-the-day routine. An old stump is still providing materiel. I resolve to return later to investigate further.

Elk Creek is swollen as I cross the Old Bridge. I continue to swing around on Huck-a-Lui Trail to the Hollow. The pond has nearly reached the Throne, and is no longer a pond, having joined the now rushing waters of the swollen creek. I look over toward the Swing, and it is being swallowed by the Creek. I make a quick rescue of the Swing and tuck it among the branches of the Poplar tree for the winter.

I continue with my log from the quarry toward the Falls. The Falls are gone, replaced by the swollen creek, but the banks are not breeched here. I continue up to the Knoll, and place the log by the hammock there. A nice foot rest.

Continuing to the Confluence, I see that it has disappeared as well under the overflowing creek. The creek has morphed into a small river.

Swing in distress.

The Hollow has undergone its first disaster, but come out essentially unscathed.

October, 2021

Sunday, October 3, 2021

I guide Nadine and Heather back toward the Industrial Complex discovered on Thursday. Entering the hidden pathway I lead them back toward the quarry, but suddenly the path seems to disappear. We all remark on the Blair Witch Project. I retreat and we go to the Hollow instead where I show them the Environs. Heather appears perplexed.

Tuesday, October 5, 2021

Buck emails me: he's enthusiastically read the books and wants to chat, mentioning that he has not done much recreational hiking. He's a maker of trails, not a consumer.

I immediately reply that we might consider Mt. Olympus in the spring. He jumps on the idea. I go to recreation.gov to see about 2021 wilderness permits and they are not yet available.

In the spirit of customer service, I return to the Industrial Complex to see why the trail disappeared, and the problem immediately is manifest: I had been wearing sunglasses! With regular glassed on, the trail is obvious. I relocated some fallen branches to make it even more navigable, then grab a beautiful piece of harvested wood that was lying about, and put it at the entrance to the Industrial Complex as a sign for any future visitor.

Monday, October 11, 2021

Ron and I returned from a backpacking trip to the High Divide this past weekend. We take a quick visit to the Hollow in the morning. It is a cool morning, but not the wintry mix we encountered at our campsite the previous morning.

Making our way along the wrong-way on Buck Lake #4, we arrive in due course. The Old Bridge, as for all, is an obstacle, but no events this time. Ron sees the first of the many directional signs in the Hollow and is naturally impressed. We make our way down the easy path to the Hollow. Once there, he inspects the quality of the Throne and immediately traipses over to the Landing to inspect the winter quarters of the Swing. The Creek is at a normal height.

Ron at the Hollow.

We then wend along the Creek to Nadine Falls. The trickle is as usual: the Creek has absorbed the recent rains without overflowing its normal banks. We then make the quick climb to Isabella Knoll where I point out the advantages from that prospect, including the conversation pit, and then we wind up the Huck-a-Lui trail and back to the Hollow. Ron wants to map the return trip on his GPS.

Suddenly, Ron spies a large stump at the point where the trail to the Hollow offers an alternate route to the Falls. He declares, "We need a library here." He elaborates about the various volumes of literature related to Ron's Hollow that could be stuffed into a small, over-sized bird-house there. I'm intrigued. But, this is a significant change to the Hollow, I rejoin. Certainly, the cultural level would be elevated and the presence of an institution of higher learning might attract all manner of ingratiates. We agree it's a good idea. Budget constraints in mind, I figure my best bet is Etsy or Amazon. This is above my engineering pay-grade.

We return to the Village by the route we arrived by: Buck Lake #4. We talk about the possible loss of the Hollow to memory, then a sudden discovery by some random adventurer a hundred years distant. What will they think? What will the world be like? Will the library still be there?

Later that morning, Ron leaves for his eventual return to Wisconsin, taking draft copies of "Ron's Hollow" and "Olympics from the Pacific" with him. For me there is a deep sadness as we fist-bump a good-bye. I was a bit sneezy in the morning, so hugs are out of the question.

I imagine few trips back to the Hollow as winter approaches and the rains increase. Perhaps a Hollow by the fireplace will be my sanctuary over the months as the Wet Woods gather in the moisture that assures their grandeur and endurance.

Appendix C: Original maps

Appendix D: DNR bike trails

Appendix E: Glossary

Bike Trails: A system of easy to difficult mountain bike trails designed by Buck and built by the Evergreen Trails Association on the Washington Department of Natural Resources land behind (to the east of) the Village.

Buck Lake: The junction of the Buck Lake #1 and Buck Lake #4 trails, as well as the Service Trail.

Cornnubbin: Short for "Her Majesty Queen of the Cornnubbins Protector of Hollows", aka my granddaughter.

Cornnubbin Confluence: The junction of Elk Creek with an anonymous smaller creek.

Cornnubbins: (plural) Any of several of the Cornnubbin type, typified by shrunken heads and out-sized voices signifying nothing.

Creek: See "Elk Creek."

Elk Creek: A sleepy creek in the Northwest of the Olympic Peninsula near the Village.

Environs: The general vicinity of the Hollow.

Gabe's Grotto: Location of the Treasure.

Grandpa Jack Tree: The splintered by living old Hemlock on Isabella Knoll.

Grandpa Tom Tree: The Western Hemlock shading the Hollow.

Hollow: See "Ron's Hollow."

Isabella Knoll: The miniature hill to the east of Nadine Falls, providing a prospect over the Falls.

Landing: On the far side of Grandpa Tom Tree from the Throne, the Landing is the best place to get on the Swing. The New Bridge from the North Bank has its southern end here.

Nadine Falls: The subtle waterfall between the Hollow and Isabella Knoll on the Creek.

New Bridge: Presently a log of dubious structural integrity underneath the Swing.

North Bank: The alternate gateway to the Hollow leading to the New Bridge. The original and preferred entrance is via the Old Bridge.

Old Bridge: The original infrastructure spanning the Creek and leading to the Hollow.

Ron: The "ruggedly handsome" engineer who inspired the Hollow.

Ron's Hollow: The roughly triangular area bounded by Elk Creek on the north, the embankment on the southwest, and Grandpa Tom's Tree laying on the east border. See book, "Ron's Hollow."

Swing: Suspended over the Creek, the Swing is a very comfortable place to do absolutely nothing. The New Bridge is underfoot. The Swing is accessed from the Landing.

Terry's Tree: The unassuming but noble hemlock between the Hollow and the Falls.

Throne: The royal seat in the Hollow.

Treasure: A collection of items of great worth and inestimable value.

Village: the town of Seabrook, which resembles a village.

The author grew up near Chicago and now lives near Ron's Hollow with Nadine, and dogs Stan and Bell. His other books include:

- Olympics via the Pacific: Four Epic Hikes in the Wet Woods
- Bull Beaches: A Dog's Guide to the Olympic Coast
- Ghosts & Salmon: Suffering in the Wet Woods
- Darkest Winter: Journal of a Pandemic